BASICS

SITE MANAGEMENT

\\ LARS-PHILLIP RUSCH

BASICS

SITE MANAGEMENT

BIRKHÄUSER
BASEL · BOSTON · BERLIN

CONTENTS

.

FOREWORD

Quality control during the process of turning plans into an actual building is one of the architect's most important tasks. The requirements formulated in the design must be translated into real constructions and building elements on the basis of implementation plans and tenders. This means that during the implementation phase, the architect must systematically manage and monitor the quality of construction and ensure that targets are reached despite any unforeseen events. It is in this phase that the level of constructional quality represented by the building in the longer term and enjoyed by its users is ultimately determined. Apart from the quality of construction, the most important aspects of building implementation at a general level are usually the maintenance of cost limits and deadlines – essential criteria for the client in determining the success or failure of the project.

Although periods of practical training may have provided students and those entering the profession with an initial insight into the workings of planning offices and building sites, most have little concrete experience of how building sites function. *Basics Site Management* takes this into account and provides a structured and easily understandable introduction to the various areas of work that this profession entails. The book clearly identifies the different aspects of good site management. Efficient organization of the building site, a functioning schedule, systematic cost management, constant monitoring of the implementation quality and a professional procedure for handing over the finished building to the client: all essential tools for the successful site manager.

Of course, this book cannot be a substitute for real practical experience. Nevertheless, the practically oriented and structured introduction it provides to the fundamental tasks and interconnected aspects of site management offers a solid foundation for the effective and rapid transition into this professional field.

Bert Bielefeld
Editor

INTRODUCTION

Site management begins when the time comes to translate abstract plans and texts into their precise physical counterparts on the building site. Experiencing the process by which the planned building first takes on form as a shell, and then is progressively turned into something that previously only existed on paper or as a model, is often laborious but always instructive.

Successful site management is measured in terms of its capacity to meet targets in the three most important categories: costs, schedules, and quality. If costs remain within the agreed limits, if the building is finished within the agreed time frame, and if the quality of the building meets the client's requirements, the site manager will have successfully completed the project. › Fig. 1

During the building process, the site manager therefore has to control factors that influence costs, schedules and quality such that deviations remain within agreed limits, can be offset as the project progresses or can be agreed with the client.

Once the design, planning submissions and working plans have been completed, the results of initial invitations to tender need to be considered and the various contractors selected. For the architect and the client the phase of implementation now begins. Depending on the particular project structure, it is possible for the planning and tendering phases to overlap with the implementation phase. While details of the final structure and building services equipment are still being honed in the architectural office, the building shell is already taking shape on the site. › Fig. 2

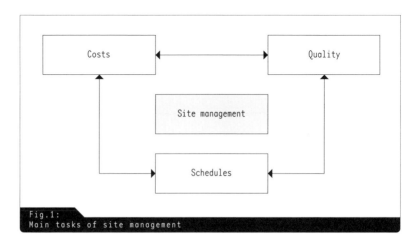

Fig.1:
Main tasks of site management

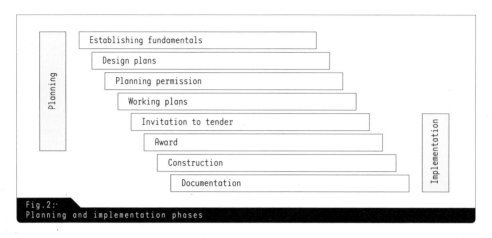

Fig.2:
Planning and implementation phases

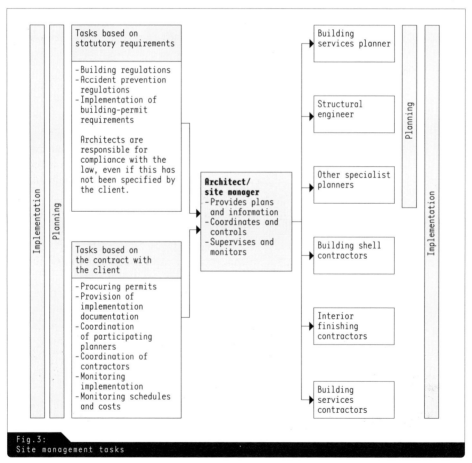

Fig.3:
Site management tasks

FUNDAMENTALS OF SITE MANAGEMENT

PREPARING SITE MANAGEMENT

Monitoring
construction
for the client

The terms site management and site manager are often understood in the practical context as relating to different functions. On the one hand, the site manager is contractually responsible for monitoring the construction process, for checking that the wishes of the client are being professionally and properly implemented (i.e. according to the agreed plans) by the various contractors. Apart from the actual architectural design, this process includes a range of other agreements made during the planning phase, for example with regard to construction costs and schedules, which must be implemented by the site manager in the course of building.

Monitoring
statutory pro-
visions

On the other hand, the site manager also has to ensure that the statutory provisions set down by building authorities are adhered to. The site manager is responsible for plans being realized in the form that has been given official approval. In addition, the site manager is responsible for ensuring safety standards are maintained in the construction process, and that the site does not pose any threat to the safety of those working on the project or anyone else. > Fig. 3

THE MOMENT OF TRUTH

The implementation of architectural plans is the real "moment of truth." At this point it becomes clear whether the envisaged construction can actually be built. Every architect should take the opportunity to experience this process, because the actual construction process can be an invaluable source of ideas for the development of other projects. As already stated, the tasks of the site manager include monitoring costs, schedules and quality. As a rule, the work required here is detailed in the fee structure for planning services. The architect's task is not an arbitrary one; it is the "bringing into being" of a building that accords with planning and is technically and functionally free of faults.

It is particularly important to bear in mind that construction always involves the production of varying objects under varying conditions. In contrast to factory-based forms of production such as automobile manufacturing, building projects are characterized by a range of features:

_ The scope of the project, the available time and the required quality differ from case to case.
_ The project comprises activities that are limited in terms of space and time.
_ The location of the project is different in each case, and each has its own features.

_ The cooperation of a large number of people/firms is required who have (often) not worked together before and who will (probably) not work together again.

_ As a rule, the participants have contradictory interests (managing the client's money as best as possible while making a profit on the contract).

_ Success needs to be achieved directly. There is no scope for "practice" prior to carrying out the project. Although some projects may be based on prototypes, there is no such thing as a "pilot run".

_ Targets and results cannot usually be negotiated in retrospect (particularly deadlines).

QUALITY SPECIFICATIONS

Since site management is primarily concerned with realizing the client's wishes as set out in the tender specifications, it is these specifications that form the basis of all activities falling within the site manager's area of responsibility.

Tender specifications
> 𝕀

Depending on the type of tender, tender specifications can describe all required work in detail (detailed tender) or the targeted performance of the end result (functional tender).

If the award, i.e. the commissioning of contractors, has been made on the basis of detailed tender specifications, the site manager can usually rely on the details regarding building quality and quantities that have been agreed and defined in these specifications. Nevertheless, he or she should – as with all other relevant documentation – check that these details are correct and complete.

> ✎

The scope of services is precisely defined in the course of implementation planning and tendering specification. If the tender is based on a functional tender, i.e. the desired result is functionally defined by the tender specifications, the contracted firm is free to choose the building procedure and the details of its implementation. In this case, site management is limited to checking the quality of work as specified in the functional specification.

Agency site management

Since in the case of functional tender specifications a contract is usually awarded to the relevant building firm early in the planning process, the firm in question assumes responsibility for further detailed planning and the supervision of implementation. However, clients still require site managers who can act as their advocates and monitor the work of the contracted firm. Even if the building firm is coordinating itself in this situation, it must adhere to the prevailing regulations and standards. The supervising role of the architect is therefore often referred to as "agency site management" in this context.

12

SCHEDULE SPECIFICATIONS

Apart from ensuring that the required quality is achieved and that costs remain within the framework set by the client › Chapter Cost specifications the site manager is responsible for the completion of the project on schedule. As a rule, the completion date is set at an early stage of planning and is no longer negotiable once building and the task of site management have commenced. For the client, meeting the deadline for completion can be extremely important. For example, failure to meet completion deadlines can mean enormous costs in unpaid rents on large commercial properties.

Framework time schedule

The basis of site-management deadline planning is the framework time scheduling carried out by the architect, the client or the project manager. The framework time schedule covers not only the planning phase (at what point do particular plans and tenders need to be completed?) and the implementation phase from commencement to completion, but also a number of intermediate deadlines relevant for the client, such as the laying of the foundation stone, the topping-out ceremony and the date of occupation. These dates are often fixed and linked with other schedules and thus cannot be renegotiated. The planning of the construction process and the way site management can influence it are discussed in detail below. › Chapter Scheduling and implementation planning

COST SPECIFICATIONS

Apart from specifications applying to the quality of and schedule for implementation, another aspect that is particularly significant for site management is the budget prescribed by the client, i.e. the cost framework. As a rule, costs associated with the project are covered by the budget designated by the client. One consideration influencing the awarding of

---

\\ Note:
Tenders and the drawing up of tender specifications are explained in detail in *Basics Tendering* by Tim Brandt and Sebastian Franssen, Birkhäuser Publishers 2007

\\ Tip:
If the responsible site manager has been only partly involved in the production of the relevant tendering documentation or not at all, it is essential that he or she make a thorough study of the commissioned offers by the contracted firms. Only in this way is it possible to gain an overview of which firm is supposed to provide which services and the quality and quantities involved as well as where there are interfaces with other specifications and contractors.

contracts is thus ensuring that adequate funds will be available during the actual building process. Budget planning should also normally include a certain buffer to cover any unforeseen contingencies arising in the course of building. Nevertheless, a particularly important task of site management is ensuring the prescribed cost framework is adhered to. The site manager is not entitled to enter into agreements that can be disadvantageous for the client. This particularly applies to undertakings to contractors that will result in cost overruns. As one slogan puts it: "The architect's mandate ends where the client's purse begins."

As shown in Figure 4, in the course of construction, the site manager gains an increasingly precise overview of what the building will ultimately cost. It is imperative that the client is kept informed about the development of project costs. › Chapter Cost management

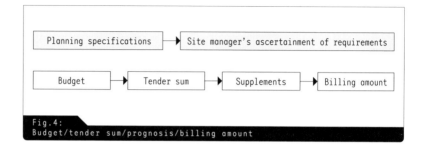

Fig.4:
Budget/tender sum/prognosis/billing amount

ORGANIZING THE BUILDING SITE

In addition to safeguarding the client's interests, site managers are also responsible for the overall structure of operations on the building site. This involves exercising a certain amount of control over the activities of all those participating in the construction process, for example by ensuring that the necessary safety measures are put in place and are maintained, that workers are using the required protective equipment, and that the building site is kept free of clutter. The responsibility for industrial safety plays a particularly important role in the organization of building sites.

BUILDING SITE FACILITIES

The type and size of the building project involved determines the type of facilities needed in terms of cranes, storage space, accommodation, and entrances and exits. In addition to various types of large and small machinery, site facilities need to include a well planned infrastructure with access points, internal roads and storage spaces.

Equipment
_ Cranes, hoists, scaffolding
_ Barriers and safety facilities
_ Site illumination

Infrastructure
_ Storage areas for materials and components
_ Site offices, accommodation and toilets/washrooms
_ Building site paths and roads with entrances and exits
_ Connections for electricity, water, sewage and, where required, heating
_ Measures designed to protect the environment and immediate surroundings, e.g. adjacent buildings

Contractual
agreements
regarding
building site
facilities

The question of which building site facilities and equipment are to be provided by the client and which by the contractors should be covered by the tender specifications and already settled at the time contracts are agreed. In the case of large building projects, the provision of site facilities and equipment is usually detailed and commissioned as a separate service in a tendering agreement. The division of costs for facilities used by all contractors, such as washroom containers, scaffolding, electricity and water, must be contractually established and itemized in the relevant contracts.

The type of facilities and equipment used on a building site will also be influenced by the following factors:

_ Surroundings (inner city, open countryside, construction zone including other building sites, etc.)
_ Type and size of the construction project
_ Construction period
_ Time of year in which construction is taking place
_ Construction method, e.g. precast concrete sections, site-mixed concrete, prefabricated construction

The individual elements making up building site facilities and equipment are sketched in a site plan. › Fig. 5 The way in which facilities, storage and transit areas, and the building area are arranged needs to allow delivery vehicles to move within the pivot range of cranes and cranes to reach storage areas for building materials such as scaffolding, shuttering and armoring for reinforced concrete, prefabricated components, and facade elements. However, break rooms and site containers should be located

 outside this radius.

The fitness for traffic and stability of surrounding streets and open areas also need to be checked prior to beginning construction. It is often the case that temporary roads have to be built in the course of establishing a building site, and particular crane locations reinforced due to heavy

 loads.

Adapting
building site
facilities

Where conditions on a building site are cramped, it may be necessary to adapt site facilities several times in the course of the project. Further-

---

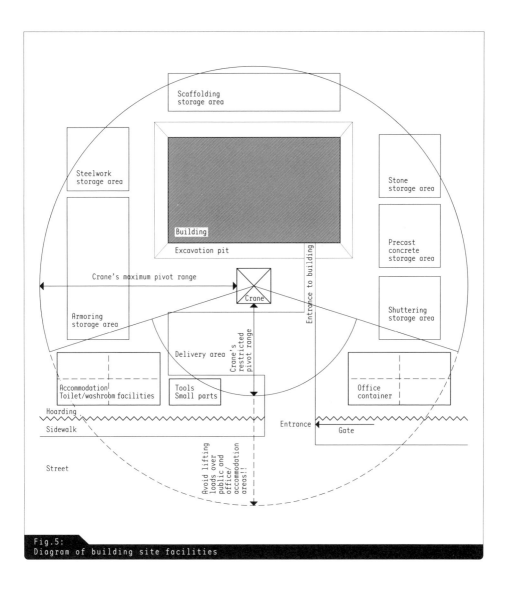

Scaffolding
storage area

Steelwork
storage area

Stone
storage area

Building

Excavation pit

Precast
concrete
storage area

Crane's maximum pivot range

Crane

Entrance to building

Armoring
storage area

Shuttering
storage area

Delivery area

Crane's
restricted
pivot range

Accommodation
Toilet/washroom facilities

Tools
Small parts

Office
container

Hoarding

Sidewalk

Entrance

Gate

Street

Avoid lifting
loads over
public and
office/
accommodation
areas!!

Fig.5:
Diagram of building site facilities

more, adapting site facilities to the various phases of construction is also a part of good economic management. For example, once the building shell and the roof have been completed, it is usually no longer necessary to have a construction crane on site. All further transport needs can be met by hoists and mobile cranes.

Building in winter requires a number of additional provisions. These include:

_ Road grit for paths and roads
_ Additional lighting for roads and walkways
_ Frost protection for water pipes
_ Heating technology to achieve the temperatures required for particular building components
_ Coverings for components (frost and general weather protection)
_ Protective housing for project sections
_ Coverings (and, where required, pre-heating technology) for building materials

In addition, site managers need to be aware of the limitations on outside work during periods of cold weather. Assessing whether work can be carried out or not requires consultation with the site managers for each of the contractors involved in the project, and safety must be the highest priority.

THE SAFENESS OF BUILDING SITES

Building sites located in urban areas present a number of dangers. Every building site must be signposted in a way that is visible by day and night and that clearly and simply indicates these dangers. > Figs 6, 7 and 8 Particularly dangerous areas must be cordoned off to prevent unauthorized entry.

Public authorities require that signage and barriers on public streets and walkways are supplemented by additional traffic signs. Moreover, optical barriers such as

_ Barrier boards
_ Warning tape
_ Cones
_ Warning beacons

must be arranged such that dangerous areas are clearly demarcated.

> ♀
>
> \\ Important:
> The site manager is responsible for ensuring
> these safety features are well maintained.
> When work finishes for the day, managers
> should tour the site to check all hoardings,
> doors and gates.

Fig.6:
Building site signage

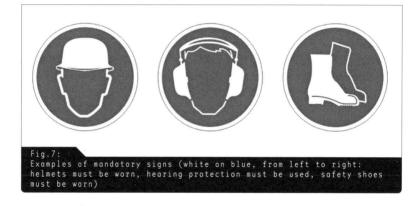

Fig.7:
Examples of mandatory signs (white on blue, from left to right: helmets must be worn, hearing protection must be used, safety shoes must be worn)

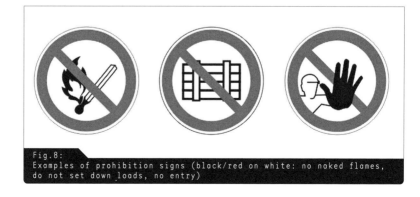

Fig.8:
Examples of prohibition signs (black/red on white: no naked flames, do not set down loads, no entry)

19

Fig.9:
Building site facilities in London

Walkways on the building site should be constructed with safety in mind and, where applicable, equipped with railings. Public walkways adjacent to the building site must be protected in such a way that the site cannot present any threat whatsoever. This may involve completely covering walkways or blocking and rerouting them. › Fig. 9

Industrial safety on the building site

Industrial safety covers not only accident prevention but also protection from occupational illnesses and other damage to health. The intensity of physical work on a building site and the use of dangerous materials, machines and tools mean that a well-organized occupational health and safety regime is essential. Due to their importance, the principles and organization of occupational health and safety are regulated by a range of laws and ordinances. These regulations deal with

_ The internal organization of and responsibility for occupational health and safety within building firms
_ The involvement of other organizations in occupational health and safety
_ The client's responsibilities

Responsibility on the building site

Occupational
health and
safety
coordinator

The client is obligated to institute and implement occupational health and safety measures both during the planning of a building project and in the context of construction itself. Since very few clients are in a position to meet this obligation, the task is usually passed to the site manager. Where required, site managers will engage an occupational health and safety coordinator, or HSC, to assist in this task. In Europe, for example, EU guidelines require the involvement of an HSC in all large-scale building sites. The responsibilities involved, whether carried out by the site manager or HSC, include:

_ Adhering to the principles of occupational health and safety in implementation planning
_ Notifying authorities about the project
_ Drawing up a health and safety plan in the case of large building sites and/or particularly dangerous work
_ Compiling health and safety documentation for later work on the completed building

\\Tip:
In cases where walkways and/or streets near the building site have to be blocked for several hours or even days to allow for the delivery and assembly of large building components, approval must be obtained from local authorities. Adequate information regarding such occurrences should also be displayed for local residents and pedestrians several days in advance.

As a rule, the site manager and the HSC also draw up instructions regarding the specificities of the building site. These contain information on access roads, building electricity and water, safety regulations, areas of work, etc., and should be documented in reports.

Maintaining and enforcing safety regulations on building sites is particularly important to the site manager. If contravention of these regulations results in an accident, the site manager is personally liable. Such cases involve what is known as breach of duty, an offence also committed by anyone who:

_ Fails to give requisite instructions
_ Fails to carry out checks
_ Fails to stop wrong conduct despite the possibility of doing so
_ Fails to report shortcomings they are unable to handle
_ Fails to use provided safety equipment

Breaches of duty give rise to liability claims when:

_ The result is damage to persons or property
_ Such breaches contravene prevailing laws
_ Personal fault is proved
_ The task involved is within the field of personal responsibility
_ The breach involves an individual acting or failing to act in a way that has caused the damage.

The safety and health plan (SHP) is one of the most important documents relating to occupational health and safety on the building site. It must be readable and understandable by all people working on the site. The plan describes the dangers that can arise during the building process and the ways of countering them, e.g. using the required safety equipment. This information is categorized by trade. Dangers arising as a result of the need to coordinate different types of work within the same time frame are also listed. The health and safety plan is based on the scheduling and implementation plan.

Should an accident occur on a building site, the provision of first aid must be guaranteed. Organizing the first aid system should cover the following aspects:

_ First aid facilities and resources, i.e. first aid kits, stretchers and, where appropriate, a first aid room
_ Identification of the site's first aider by name and location

_ Visible display of "first aid instructions" including telephone numbers and addresses of emergency medical services, the local hospital and the local emergency doctor

The scope of the required facilities and resources will depend on the size of the building site.

Contractors' responsibilities
Contracted firms are required by law to protect their employees from dangers to life and health. Responsibility for ensuring that this obligation is met is usually assumed by someone with a supervisory role on the building site, and adherence to statutory requirements is also monitored by the client's site manager.

An effective occupational health and safety regime can only be established on building sites if all participants cooperate and a range of measures are coordinated. These include arranging work stations, machinery and tools so that they are completely safe or risk is minor. If this is not possible, personal protective measures should also be taken. All risk factors should be pointed out on easily comprehensible signs. › Figs 7 and 8 Where several firms are working simultaneously on a building site, additional measures are required. For instance, firms need to inform each other about work that presents a risk for all parties and coordinate appropriate safety measures. This information exchange should take place in site meetings and also on the site itself. › Chapter Organizing the building site, Site meeting

COOPERATION ON THE BUILDING SITE
Site management means dealing with people with different interests, different levels and types of education and, in some cases, from different countries. The site manager not only represents the client but is also responsible for the coordination of the building site. For this reason the site manager often has to act as a moderator on the site and make clear and responsible decisions regarding questions that arise, for instance, between specialist planners or contractors. In this function the site manager is able to issue directives and has authority over contractors. The contractual relationships between the client, the site manager and the contracted firms are shown schematically in Figure 10.

Other site
managers

As already indicated, depending on the type of building project and contract, other planners and specialists may also be involved in supervising firms contracted by the client and, where required, coordinating their different areas of work. › Chapter Quality management, Monitoring and safeguarding quality However, responsibility for overall coordination lies with the supervising architect. The other "site managers" working on the site

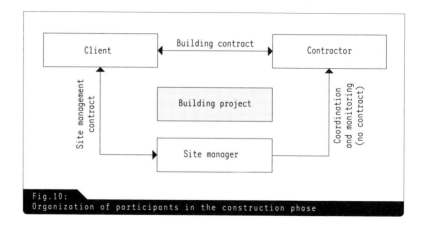

Fig.10:
Organization of participants in the construction phase

are designated in terms of their function. Unfortunately these titles are not always used uniformly:

_ Site architect/site manager: an architect or construction engineer commissioned by the client to manage a construction project (this is the person referred to in this book as the site manager)
_ Specialist engineer: specialized planner commissioned by the client to manage construction in a particular trade area, e.g. building services
_ Company site manager: staff member of contracting firm with a supervisory role. In situations involving several site supervisors there is usually also a senior site manager with overall responsibility.

Figure 11 shows a possible organizational structure for participants in the building phase.

Building
contracts

In addition to safety, the basis of cooperation on the building site is provided by the building contracts. As a rule, tender specifications provide a basis for building implementation in the form of the regulations, guidelines and standards applying to the respective trades, which are described and contractually agreed. Building contracts can include further details relating to the construction process, particularly concerning schedules, methods of payment, and possible contractual penalties if deadlines are exceeded. In addition, contractors are generally expected to:

_ Carry out their work as contractually specified on their own responsibility and on their own account

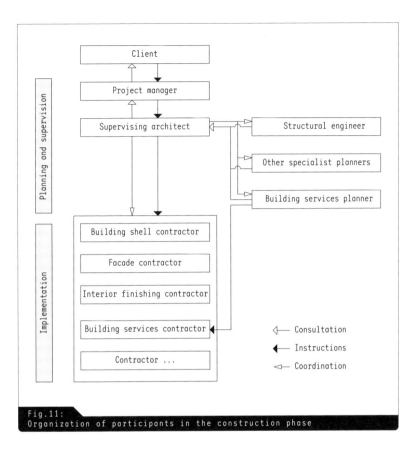

Fig.11:
Organization of participants in the construction phase

_ Adhere to statutory provisions
_ Fulfill obligations to the client imposed by law, government authorities and trade organizations
_ Provide for order in the workplace
_ Communicate in writing any misgivings they may have concerning the proposed form of implementation, materials or components provided by the client or work by other contractors
_ Protect their work from damage and theft up until final inspection
_ Remedy any defects in their work detected by the client prior to and during final inspection
_ Comply with scheduled deadlines.

Of course, contractual agreements also give contractors rights in relation to the client. For instance, the contractor has the right to demand sufficient security for advance risk. If the contractor's services require financial investment in building materials, for example, he or she is entitled to demand proof that the client is able to pay the contractually agreed costs.

The organization or hierarchy of contractors is basically similar for all trades. The company site manager and the technical supervisor are the contact persons for the site manager. They are present at site meetings and are responsible for coordinating their company's employees and subcontractors, and to their own firm's management for the economical implementation of planning. In turn, the foremen are responsible for their respective crews.

On almost all building sites it is common practice for contractors to commission other firms, called subcontractors, to carry out work they cannot or do not want to do themselves. There is no contractual relationship between the client and subcontractors, and the respective contractor is responsible for all commissioning, implementation, payment, and warranties relating to its subcontractors. However, the engagement of such subcontractors does require the client's approval.

Systematizing site management documents

It is important to have all site management documents ready to hand. The content of this documentation will depend on the nature of the building project and how far it has progressed. In order to maintain an overview of the flood of correspondence, reports, plans and notes, a system of folders should be used. This system can be structured as follows:

_ Folder 0: Current planning documents with plan list and plan receipt and delivery
_ Folder 1: Building permit documents and related correspondence
_ Folder 2: Correspondence with client
_ Folder 3: Correspondence with specialist planners
  _ Folder 3.1: Structural engineering
  _ Folder 3.2: Building services planning
  _ Folder 3.3: Fire security
  _ Folder 3.4: ...
_ Folder 4: Project manager
_ Folder 5: Contractors with respective tender specification, building contract, correspondence, invoices, planning documents, bill of quantities, etc.

_ Folder 5.1: Building shell
_ Folder 5.2: Building services (BS)
_ Folder 5.3: Plastering
_ Folder 5.4: Screed work
_ Folder 5.5: ...
_ Folder 6: Site meeting / project meeting reports
_ Folder 7: Delivery notes, certification reports, supporting documents
_ Folder 8: Construction diary – site management
_ Folder 9: Construction diary – contractors
_ Folder 10: ...

Construction diary

In order to be able to comprehend which work has been carried out and when, which contractors were on the building site with how many workers, or whether there have been any notable incidents, the site manager must keep a construction diary. › Fig. 12 The construction diary should be updated daily and as well as structural descriptions should contain the following information:

_ Date
_ Weather (temperature, cloud cover, rainfall)
_ Trades represented on the building site (carpenters, masons,...)
_ Number of workers present from each firm; if applicable, supervising foremen
_ Notes describing work carried out
_ Tools/machinery utilized
_ Particular materials used (e.g. paints, primers)
_ Particular components installed
_ Installation and operating instructions for installed devices – as appendix
_ Documentation of actual or suspected defects and damage
_ Progress of construction work in general (overview) and in detail
_ Working plans given to contractors
_ If applicable, missing plans
_ Agreed changes to plans

A range of forms are available for contractors to use for their construction diaries. › Fig. 13 Where possible, the site manager should also have forms made up that are tailored to the particular construction site. Contractors are usually contractually obliged to keep a construction diary, which must be handed to the site manager at agreed intervals.

Construction diary building 55		Mo	Tu	We	Th	Fr	Sa	Su
Date	05.06.2006							
Weather	Sunny							
Min°C	20				x			
Max°C	30							

Firms present:					Workers			
1	R&P				11			
2	Acoustics firm				8			
3	Miller,sanitary installation				15			
4	Smith,electrical installation				4			
5	Facade				8			
6	Walthers metalwork				5			
7	Roofing				3			
8	BMA				4			
9	Painting				3			
10	Screed				2			

Work performed:

1 Kitchen, toilet cores walled off, preparation for screed in kitchen
2 Plasterboard floors 4–6, kitchen ceiling
3 Kitchen installations, heating circuits, heaters 4th/5th floors
4 Electrical installations kitchen, core 10–11, office areas
5 Office facade floors 4–6, glazing floors 4–5, Office facade attachments
6 Canteen handrail, stairways 5–7, brackets stairways 5–7
7 Canteen roof sealed, remaining work on office roof
8 Kitchen installations area
9 Painting technical rooms, office balustrades, stairwells 10–11
10 Screed work basement

Visits to building site:

Directives:

Mr. Miller, fire prevention measures: removal of all fire loads (packaging, palettes, topping out wreath, etc.) from the building site. Hire fire risk from welding work.
Repair emergency drainage (R&P)

To be noted:

Heavy rain over night
Roof of 2nd construction section leaky
Emergency drainage damaged

Fig.12:
Page from site manager's construction diary

Construction diary

Construction diary Day: 05.06.06		Building site: Building 55	Page number: 34862	
Supervisor: Walthers / Miller Foreman: Galbraith / Smith		Weather: sunny	max.: 20 °C min.: 30 °C	

Labor deployment

	Number	Total hours
Supervisors	2	11
Foremen		
Skilled craftsmen	7	60
Machine operators		
Metal workers		
Laborers	2	17
Total	11	88

Machinery deployment

Contractual services

Job no.	Quantity	Text	Costs
		Brickwork done in bathrooms axis 4–6 d=9.5cm in pumice on 2nd floor	
		F90 brick walls done axis 9–10 on 6th floor d=11.5cm in limestone	
		Installation walls done on 5th and 6th floors axis 4–6 in aerated concrete	
		Toilet tanks and piping embedded in wall	

Non-contractual services

Forms stripped on foundation for installation walls in bathrooms axis 4–6 3rd–5th floor.

Doorway in wall on 3rd floor axis 9 chiseled out and rubble removed

Other + checks

Emergency drainage checked and repaired

Rennemann	Rusch
Signature R&P	for the client

PROJECT MEETING/SITE MEETING

Complex building projects require the cooperation of all those involved. Depending on the task at hand, the site manager can make use of different tools to facilitate such cooperation. These tools include:

_ Project meetings
_ Site meetings
_ Reports
_ Face-to-face discussions
_ Letter, fax, e-mail
_ Telephone consultation
_ Photographic documentation
_ Sketches and drawings
_ Workflow and cost charts
_ Construction site inspection/site survey

Although all relevant agreements have been formally established in the building contracts, it may well be necessary to reach further agreements during the construction process itself. Since such agreements often involve detailed coordination between the different trades, they are made in the context of project and site meetings. › Figs 14 and 15 Agreements detailed in meeting reports are binding and, depending on the specific agreement, have contractual status regarding subsequent work. Table 1 provides an overview of how such meetings can be productively organized.

Project meeting   Project and site meetings should be held at regular intervals. Along with the site manager, project meetings involve the project manager (if this is not the same person as the site manager), the client, the project supervisor, and, if required, the project and site managers attached to other specialist planners working on the project. In the project meeting the client is informed about the current situation on the building site regarding the progress of planning and construction, cost developments and schedules. If required, the meeting is also used to make decisions on changes relating to schedules, costs or quality. If decisions are required that can only be made by the client, the relevant information must be compiled and presented by the site manager in a way that facilitates quick and clear decision-making.

Site meeting   At the request of the contracted firms, the site manager must organize a regular site meeting. Site meetings involve the specialist engineers engaged on the site and the site managers representing the different contractors. In the early and latter stages of the building phase, meetings often only take place once a fortnight but may be required weekly during the main building period. One element of the site meeting is a collective

Fig. 14

Project: new building, Swiss Re Headquarters, London		Participation required/Invitation	present	from – to	Ref.
Site meeting no. 12: Invitation/Report					
Date: 03.07.2007		Client — x			
		Architect — x			
Location: Building site, site management container		Site manager BS — x			
		Site manager GC — x			
Begins: 9 a.m.		SC building shell — x			
		SC interior finishing — x			
Ends: midday		SC sanitary facilities — x			
		SC ventilation			
Distribution list: as per participant list		SC electrical — x			
Additional: ☒					

Invitation			Report	Execution
Agenda item	Prepared by	Goal		
Check correspondence since 18.06.07	GC	Identical documents		
Effect of flood damage on schedule	GC SC interior finishing	Assessment delay/speedup		
Inspect interior finishing quality	GC SC interior finishing SC sanitary facilities	Assessment execution		
etc.				

Fig.14:
Example of site meeting invitation

Fig. 15

Project: new building, Swiss Re Headquarters, London		Participation required/Invitation	present	from – to	Ref.
Site meeting no. 12: Invitation/Report					
Date: 03.07.2007		Client — x	x		SD
		Architect — x	x		FD
Location: Building site, site management container		Site manager BS — x	x	10:00–11:00	KL
		Site manager GC — x	x		OL
Begins: 9 a.m.		SC building shell — x	x		WS
		SC interior finishing — x	x		AS
Ends: midday		SC sanitary facilities — x	x		VE
		SC ventilation			
Distribution list: as per participant list		SC electrical — x	x	10:30–11:00	TH
Additional: ☒					

Invitation			Report	Execution	
Agenda item	Prepared by	Goal	Assessment Result Agreement	Who	Date
Check correspondence since 18.06.07	GC	Identical documents	Assessment Result Agreement	GC and all SC	until 05.07.07
Effect of flood damage on schedule	GC SC Interior finishing	Assessment delay/speedup	Architect receives copy of encroachment complaint of 14.06.07	Client and GC	until 07.07.07
Inspect interior finishing quality	GC SC interior finishing SC sanitary facilities	Assessment execution	Client inspects (together with architect)	Client and architect	until 10.07.07
etc.					

Fig.15:
Example of an invitation also functioning as a meeting report

Tab.1: Principles for organizing project and site meetings	
Basic questions	Is this meeting needed or are there better ways of solving the problem? (What would happen without this consultation session?) Does the achievable effect justify the effort involved (lost working time for all parties)?
Goal of the meeting	Meetings should only be called when they have a concrete goal(s). Is the meeting only of value for the site manager or is it important for all participants? What results can be expected?
Preparation for the meeting	Fix agenda, identify key points Set out goals in writing Decide on procedure Determine who is responsible for the preparation of individual points Who is required to participate? Must every participant be present for the discussion of each point? Distribute agenda with invitation
Organization of the meeting	Limit participation to the necessary parties If required, organize individual discussions Provide agenda in advance and keep to it
Meeting management	Timed is saved by well chaired meetings Maintain focus on the goal Keep an eye on the time allotment Avoid peripheral issues — maintain the central focus Do not allow one-on-one discussions to develop in larger meetings Aim for consensus
Results/meeting report	Select a suitable form of meeting reports (should reports record results or the course of discussion?) Write up report soon after the meeting Clearly identify responsible parties in the meeting report Ensure clear agreement on deadlines is included in report

inspection of the building site. Detailed questions on implementation or coordination between different trades can often only be dealt with in situ.

The form of the meeting invitations and reports should provide a clear overview of all relevant points. A form should be chosen that allows for systematic and rapid reporting of results. Each participant should receive a tabularized overview of all agenda items. › Fig. 14 The example below illustrates how the results of the meeting can be entered directly into the table. › Fig. 15 In the simplest case, each participant receives a copy of this report at the end of the meeting. Only where more complex issues are involved will supplementary material be added to the report later. Such material should include explanatory sketches, photos, and data sheets.

In all cases, the invitation and the report should include the following details:

_ Construction project concerned
_ Work specifications / trades
_ Meeting location (for on-site meetings, indicate whether the site will be inspected or discussions will be confined to the site office)
_ Beginning, end
_ Participants (if required, functions and scope of authority)
_ Report distribution list (e.g. including third parties not present at the meeting and definition of internal distribution)
_ Record of topics discussed (participants may select which topics they wish to make a note of)
_ Type of agenda items (e.g. information, agreement, approval, preparation for a decision)
_ Basis of meeting (plans, reports, etc.)

\\ Tip:
When taking part in site inspections, site
managers should carry a folder containing
the relevant plans (if necessary, reduced in
size). Taking pictures with a digital camera
can also be useful for supplementing reports
and documentation. Other useful tools include
a cellular phone, a folding rule, a Dictaphone
if applicable and of course all requisite
protective equipment such as safety shoes and
helmets.

Reports on meeting results must include the relevant goal, deadline, and responsible parties. Particularly important reports have to be signed by the participants. Such reports (e.g. concerning negotiations and final inspections) should clearly indicate the number of pages involved.

Tab.2: Communication problems			
said	does not mean	→	heard
heard	does not mean	→	understood
understood	does not mean	→	agreed
agreed	does not mean	→	applied
applied	does not mean	→	maintained

\\ Note:
Even if the a generally friendly atmosphere predominates on a building site, ambiguity must be strictly avoided in meeting and final inspection reports, as it must be in all agreements relating to costs and schedules. If disagreements arise, the previously friendly atmosphere will be of little help. Written agreements are then all that can be relied on.

SCHEDULING AND IMPLEMENTATION PLANNING

Scheduling and implementation planning are two of the site manager's most important tasks. It entails identifying all deadlines relevant to the construction process and coordinating all implementation procedures in terms of technology, space and time. This requires a degree of experience in the building field. However, due to the many factors influencing the actual process of construction, there will always be deviations from the original plans.

In order to be able to meet planned deadlines, it is particularly important that one receives information on possible schedule deviations in time to adapt building procedures accordingly. The earlier deviations are recognized, the more possibilities there are to offset them. Scheduling and implementation planning as well as their management constitute one of the three main tasks of site management. The ability to complete a project within the designated time frame is a key factor in assessing the site manager's performance.

TERMS RELATING TO SCHEDULING AND IMPLEMENTATION PLANNING

All scheduling consists of processes and events as well as their relationship to one another.

Process

A process is understood as an occurrence that is defined by a beginning, duration and an end. A typical process within a schedule would be, for example, painting.

Event/
milestone

An event is an element of implementation that is not assigned a duration. Particularly important events are characterized as milestones and integrated into the schedule. Examples of milestones are the commencement and completion of building and, within the course of construction, the completion of the building shell.

Important events
for the client

In the course of almost every building project, milestones are reached that are particularly significant for the client.

Ground-breaking
ceremony

The symbolic breaking of the ground on a site marks the beginning of the construction phase. In the case of large building projects that are important for the public, the owner invites the later users or tenants of the building and official representatives of the political and business spheres to the ground-breaking ceremony.

Laying the foun-
dation stone

The laying of the foundation stone usually takes place following the completion of the excavation pit and prior to the initial cement work. In some cases a capsule containing markers of the time at which the building was constructed, such as newspapers, photos of the site or a few coins, is deposited inside the stone, which will later lie under the completed building.

Topping-out
ceremony

The topping-out ceremony is held when the shell and roof truss of the new building have been completed. Different ceremonies are held in different regions to wish the building and its owner luck. The topping-out ceremony is arranged by the owner in order to thank all participants for the work that has been completed.

Inauguration/
opening

Once the building is finally completed, an inauguration or opening ceremony is held. In contrast to the topping out ceremony, the opening is not linked with any fixed rituals. The owner usually thanks everyone who has contributed to the completion of the building and presents it to the public.

EXECUTION OF THE SCHEDULE AND IMPLEMENTATION PLAN

It is the task of the site manager to coordinate all firms working on the building site on the basis of the schedule and implementation plan. It must be clear to all participants which work they must complete at which point so that the following work phase can then begin. The way in which specific jobs are carried out is the responsibility of the firms concerned.

To be able to organize the overall building schedule, the site manager needs to be cognizant of all processes and procedures involved in the project and their interrelationships with one another. Building this knowledge base involves three types of planning:

Implementation
planning

The first step involves identifying and organizing all processes and events that are relevant to the construction phase. The goal is to pinpoint the interrelationships between all the relevant processes. This entails arranging all processes in a way that gives the course of construction a clear logic. Scheduling is of course an important factor here. If one wants to determine when and which firms are to be engaged on the building site, then it follows that the individual processes carried out by firms have to be arranged in a logical order.

\\ Example:
The duration of a process is defined by multiplying the quantity required (e.g. m^2 or m^3) by a performance factor. This indicates how much time is required on average to perform a certain task. The construction of a square meter of masonry, for example, is typically accorded a performance value of 1.4–2.0 h/m^2. A range of standard performance values can be found in the relevant literature, and many site managers establish their own standards on the basis of experience.

Once the relevant processes and interrelationships have been identified, the second step involves determining the possible duration of individual and combined processes on the basis of the overall time available for construction.

Scheduling essentially entails integrating the time frames defined in the time planning into the implementation planning to create a series of concrete deadlines. The beginning and ending of each process is thus clearly identified.

Representing schedule plans

Different ways of representing schedule plans can be used depending on the aim, user and/or project involved. A basic distinction is made between four types of representation: bar charts, line diagrams, network plans, and deadline lists. › Fig. 16 The bar chart is now the usual method employed for building projects.

In bar charts, processes and events are listed along the vertical axis. The horizontal axis is used as a timeline. Each process is represented by a bar, the length of which corresponds to the duration of the process. Accordingly, events and milestones are represented as processes without duration. Interdependent processes are linked by arrows. The advantages of the bar chart are that it is easy to read (even by laypersons) and its clarity. Moreover, it is a very effective means of providing an overview of an entire project. › Fig. 17

Bar charts have now become the most common method for representing schedules in the building construction field. There are numerous computer programs on the market that can be used to design schedule plans, particularly in the form of bar charts.

The simplest way of representing a schedule plan is in the form of a deadline list. Depending on the intended use and the user, different ways of representing events and processes can also be employed. When drawing up a deadline list, processes need to be characterized in such a way that they can be sorted according to different criteria, e.g. in terms of trades or construction sections. Representing interdependencies between the processes is problematic in deadline lists and requires additional annotations.

Examples of network plans and line diagrams, or volume-time diagrams, are shown in Figure 16 and will not be discussed further here since in normal building construction projects they only play a subordinate role.

Types of schedule plan

Schedule plans are distinguished in terms of their level of detail. Different levels of detail can be used in the dividing up time into months, weeks, days and even hours or in the degree to which processes are differentiated.

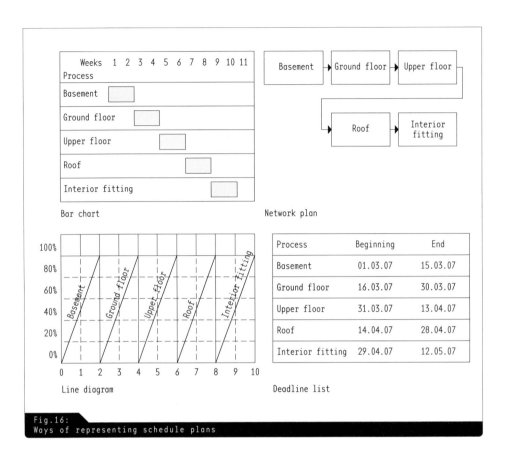

Fig.16:
Ways of representing schedule plans

Framework time
schedule   The framework time schedule is drawn up at the beginning of the
project by the client or the planner. This schedule presents the time frame
for the entire project and, as a rule, is based on the deadlines specified
by the client. These can be divided into the following very general categories:

_ Project preparation
_ Planning
_ Implementation
_ Occupation
_ Use

Master schedule   In the course of drawing up the tender specifications, the architect
usually also develops a master schedule. The deadlines contained in this
schedule are included in the tender specifications since these must be

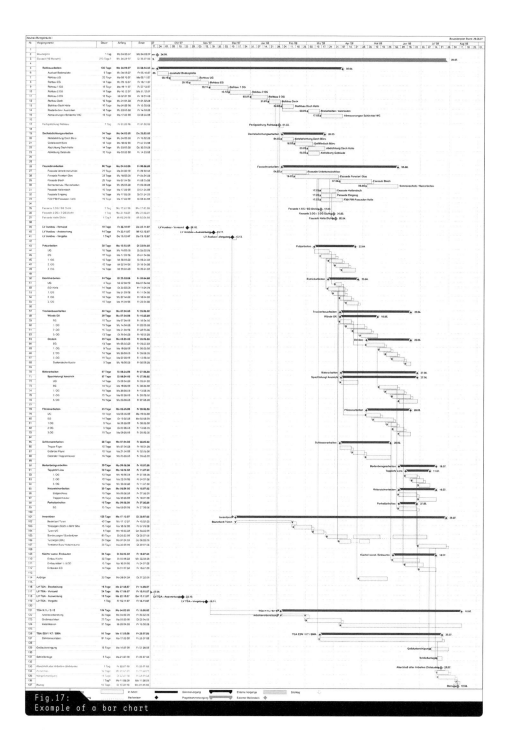

Fig.17:
Example of a bar chart

agreed contractually with the firms working on the building project. The master schedule is the foundation of the site manager's deadline planning. It is kept general, listing only the most important milestones and process or trade groups. Examples of trade groups are:

_ Preparatory measures
_ Building shell
_ Building envelope
_ Interior finishing
_ Building services
_ Final/subsequent measures

Each group comprises the trades required for that area of work. For example, the building shell group includes concrete and reinforced concrete construction, masonry work, steel construction, etc. › Tab. 3

Refined schedule

The different trade tasks are used to structure the refined schedule. If the project is divided into construction sections, the different processes are arranged in the schedule accordingly. › Chapter Scheduling and implementation planning, Schedule management The processes indicated in the refined schedule must be linked with reference to their spatial and technological interconnections. › Fig. 18

Planning processes into the refined schedule can, for example, be based on the trades and titles listed in the tender specifications. This ensures that no important processes are forgotten. A possible structure is shown in Table 3. In the additional columns the trades are assigned to the different trade groups.

P

\\ Example:
There is a technological interconnection, for example, between screed work and parquet laying. Before the parquet can be laid, the screed must have dried enough to prevent any remaining dampness from damaging the parquet. A spatial interconnection exists, for example, between painting and floor covering work, since these tasks cannot be carried out simultaneously in the same space.

Trade	Trade group				
	P	S	BE	IF	BS
Excavations	x	x			
Site preparation	x	x			
Water control work	x	x			
Waterproofing work	x				
Drainage work	x	x			
Masonry work		x			
Concrete construction work		x			
Natural stone work				x	
Concrete block work				x	
Carpentry and timber work			x		
Steel construction work		x	x		
Sealing work		x	x		
Roofing and roof-sealing work			x		
Plumbing work			x		
Dry construction work				x	
Heat insulation work			x		
Concrete conservation work		x	x		
Plastering and stucco work			x	x	
Facade work			x		
Tiling work				x	
Screed work				x	
Melted asphalt work				x	
Joinery				x	
Parquet laying				x	
Fitting work			x	x	
Roller blind work			x		
Metal construction work			x	x	
Glazing work			x	x	

Trades and assignment to trade groups (continued)

Trade	Trade group				
	P	S	BE	IF	BS
Painting and varnishing work			x		
Corrosion prevention work on steel and aluminum		x	x		
Floor covering work				x	
Wallpapering				x	
Air-conditioning installations					x
Heating and water-heating installations					x
Gas, water and drainage installations					x
Low and medium voltage electrical installations					x
Lightning protection installations					x
Conveyor systems, elevators, moving staircases/walkways					x
Building automation					x
Insulation for technical installations					x
Scaffolding		x	x		x

Abbreviations: P = preparatory work, S = shell, BE = building envelope,
IF = interior finishing, BS = building services

Detail schedule   A detail schedule can be required to coordinate work involving many workers in confined spaces or when deadlines are very tight. In a detail schedule, the time scale can be divided into units as small as hours.

> Fig. 19

\\Note:
Depending on the kind of schedule plan, related individual processes can be combined into a collective process in order to provide a clearer overview of overall procedures. Dry construction, for example, is included as a process in the refined schedule. In the detail schedule, the collective process dry construction includes the processes of framework installation, sheeting 1st side, electrical work and planking 2nd side, etc.

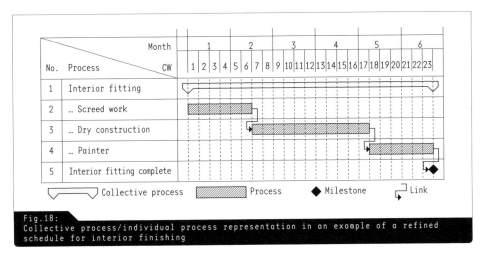

Fig.18:
Collective process/individual process representation in an example of a refined schedule for interior finishing

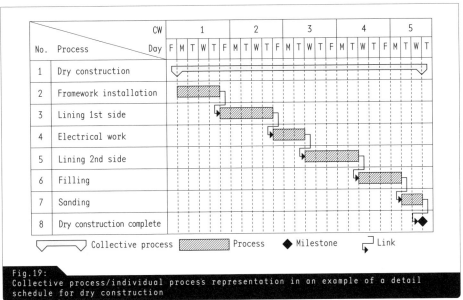

Fig.19:
Collective process/individual process representation in an example of a detail schedule for dry construction

CHECKING SCHEDULES

The date of a building's completion can be determined by a whole range of requirements. Several examples are shown in Table 4. The site manager must be aware of the reasons for the client naming a particular deadline for completion. If the deadline is linked with other fixed arrangements, it is of course not negotiable.

Building	Possible reasons for the specified deadline
Stadium	Championships
Shop/department store	Christmas shopping period
School	Beginning of school year
Highway	Beginning of holiday period
Power station	Beginning of heating period
City hall	Cost-effective building time
Factory workshop	Commencement of production (profitability analysis)

Plausibility
check of
schedule
specifications

The possibility of meeting contractual schedules should be checked by all contractual parties before signing by way of a simple plausibility check. This applies both to the site manager, who has to check the entire construction period, and to the contractors, who are responsible for determining the viability of the tasks they have been commissioned to do.

At the beginning of this checking process, the following questions should be considered:

_ Can the project be built within the time available?
_ Can all required components and materials be delivered within the building period?
_ What external factors (e.g. confined space, heavy street traffic) can influence the progress of building?

There are different ways of conducting a plausibility check. The simplest for the site manager entails comparing the current project with projects that have already been completed. The literature provides lists and overviews of finished projects. These lists include not only plans, photos and costs, but usually also time frames. Reference to comparable buildings provides a quick and simple aid for plausibility checks. If such a check shows that the requested deadline is not achievable, the client must be clearly informed.

Schedule connec-
tions between
individual
building ele-
ments or trades

In some cases, non-negotiable contractual deadlines are required not only for the final date of completion but also for individual building sections or a certain stage of construction.

In order to be able to coordinate the large number of individual trades, the site manager must also set clear deadlines for the individual contractors. Planning the individual processes within a trade is only of interest for the site manager if work by other trades is affected. This is particularly important in the case of interior finishing, since a large number of firms are working on the building site.

Obstructions

Experience shows that a whole range of changes can take place during the actual building phase. These changes can affect the quality, schedules and/or building costs. Depending on who has caused these changes, contracted firms may have the right to demand an extension of building time and associated additional costs. These claims are checked by the site manager.

Construction can be obstructed by

_ Circumstances instigated or caused by the client
_ Circumstances for which the contractor is responsible
_ Circumstances for which neither the client nor the contractor is responsible

Circumstances for which the client is responsible include:

_ Failure to secure permits
_ Failure to mark out the main axes and benchmark elevation
_ Failure by the client to make decisions e.g. on the implementation of alternative positions
_ Insufficient coordination of the contractors commissioned by the client
_ Incomplete or defective work by the architect or other planners
_ Agreed or required security not provided by client

\\ Example:
In industrial construction, machinery and larger plant are moved into the building before the outside walls or roofs are constructed. Otherwise such equipment would be too large to fit through the doors or windows of the completed building.

\\ Tip:
It is of no interest to the site manager when the building shell contractor erects the shuttering for the ground floor and builds in and cements the armoring since these processes are only carried out by the shell contractor. What is important for the site manager is that the completion deadline for the ground floor is met if, for example, plastering work is due to begin at this time.

_ Not paying as contractually specified (too late, too little)
_ Intervention by the client or architect in the planned program of building
_ Quantity increases
_ Changes in work requirements
_ Safety defects that cause building work to stop.

These circumstances can be the basis for claims by contractors against the client for deadline extensions, compensation and damages.

Apart from the reasons already listed for delays in the construction process, there are also circumstances that are the responsibility of neither the client nor the contractor. Examples include

_ A strike or lockout ordered by the employer's trade union in the contractor's or a subcontractor's field
_ Force majeure or other circumstances that the contractor cannot avoid.

Should these circumstances occur, the building contractor has a claim to an extension of building time but not to higher compensation for his or her services.

It is self-evident that the contractor cannot base claims on obstruction to work for which he or she is responsible. On the contrary, in such a situation the client may be entitled to claim damages. Several examples of possible causes for delays are summarized in Table 5.

Obstructions by other trades

> 0

If prior work done by other trades is insufficient or faulty, this needs to be brought to the attention of the client and the site manager immediately. The site manager must make clear decisions as to how these obstacles are to be eliminated.

However, the contractor is also obliged to limit the damage caused by an obstruction as far as possible. It can therefore be expected that if obstructions occur workers will move on to other necessary work rather than waiting for the obstruction to be removed.

SCHEDULE MANAGEMENT

The schedule and implementation plan allows compliance with the planned course of building to be monitored. In this context, it is important to focus in particular on processes that directly follow one another and if delayed can have a direct effect on the completion schedule. The chain formed by these processes in the schedule is referred to as the "critical path." > Fig. 20

Tools of schedule management

Effective and well-targeted schedule management requires clear identification of obstructions and consequent delays. This in turn requires

Tab.5:		
Possible causes of deviations and obstructions to the progress of work		

	Client's responsibility/ sphere of risk	Contractor's responsibility
Wrong planning and assumptions	Soil class incorrectly estimated	Productivity incorrectly estimated
	Tender-invitation for service incomplete	Incorrect machinery planned for
	Tendered quantities too small	Necessary material quantities incorrectly calculated
	Mistake in schedule	Mistake in own schedule
Interruptions to building process	Missing plans	Materials do not arrive punctually
	Lack of decisions on part of client	Machinery breaks down
	Faulty advance work by other trades	Shuttering/sheeting insufficient Building site closed due to inadequate safety measures
	Schedule overruns by authorities, architects and planners	Staff fall ill
	Unexpected archeological find	Defective quality (demolition and rebuilding)

\\Note:
Where one type of job follows on directly
from another, e.g. a dry construction wall is
painted, there is usually an inspection during
which the second trade confirms that the prior
work is of a standard that allows subsequent
work to continue without obstruction. The
site manager should make a report of this
inspection and those involved should witness
it with their signatures (see Chapter Final
inspection and acceptance).

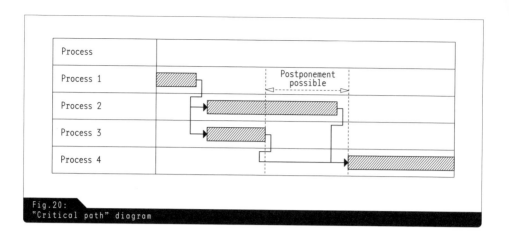

Fig.20:
"Critical path" diagram

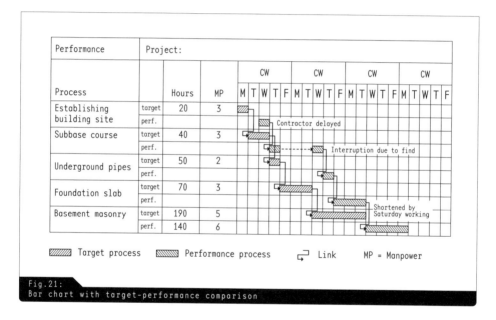

Target process · Performance process · Link · MP = Manpower

Fig.21:
Bar chart with target-performance comparison

a regular target-performance comparison to be carried out on the building site. › Fig. 21 Schedule deviations can be offset by the following measures:

_ Increase in capacity (increased workforce/increased machinery deployment)
_ Increased working time
_ Changes to building and production procedures

_ Adaptation of construction sections
_ Changes in quality

However, these measures can only offset schedule deviations to a certain degree. The costs they give rise to must be paid by the party responsible for the delay.

Increasing capacity

It is important to bear in mind that increasing capacity does not necessarily follow the rule that "What one can achieve in ten days can be achieved by ten in one day."

Often a lack of space makes it impossible to significantly increase the number of people working on a task. Workers will end up getting in each other's way, with the result that work is delayed even further.

Increasing working hours

Prolonging the working time each day or adding working days is often the simplest means of offsetting delays. Since measures for speeding up the work process normally generate additional costs, it must be clear who is to carry these costs (overtime bonuses or bonuses for work on weekends and public holidays).

Changing building procedures

Changing building procedures during construction is often only possible to a limited degree. Changes to procedures are possible, for example, in the case of:

_ Screed work: cement screed to dry screed or dry screed to melted asphalt screed
_ Plastering: wet plaster to dry plaster or thick plaster to smoothing plaster

Changes in quality

Changes in quality can also allow building procedures to be sped up or the order of procedures to be changed so that other processes are brought forward or accelerated. For one thing, such changes can result in shorter implementation times on the building site, such as when carpet is

\\Tip:
If building procedures are changed, it is important to consider the possible effects on other work sections. Using smoothing plaster or dry plaster, for example, can mean that different door frame dimensions will be required. The subsequent work sections thus have to be coordinated with the planned changes.

49

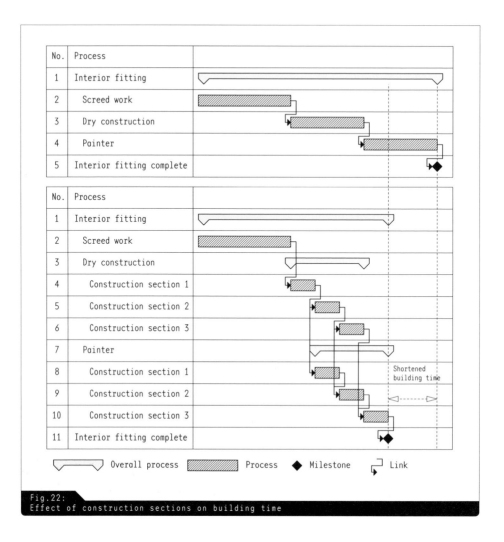

No.	Process	
1	Interior fitting	
2	Screed work	
3	Dry construction	
4	Painter	
5	Interior fitting complete	

No.	Process	
1	Interior fitting	
2	Screed work	
3	Dry construction	
4	Construction section 1	
5	Construction section 2	
6	Construction section 3	
7	Painter	
8	Construction section 1	Shortened building time
9	Construction section 2	
10	Construction section 3	
11	Interior fitting complete	

▽▽ Overall process　▨ Process　◆ Milestone　⌐ Link

Fig.22:
Effect of construction sections on building time

used instead of parquet. For another, using more rapidly available building materials can shorten supply times.

Reducing construction sections

The division of the overall project into construction sections allows the time between interdependent processes to be shortened. This is illustrated diagrammatically in Figure 22. Instead of first completing all dry construction work before commencing painting, the latter is begun as soon as the first section of dry construction work is completed. The smaller the sections, the more processes can be carried out in parallel. However, this makes planning more susceptible to disruptions because if there is a disruption in one section, the work cannot be transferred to other areas.

Fig.23:
Building using construction sections

An example of the division of a building project into construction sections can be seen in Figure 23. Shell construction, facade work and interior finishing take place in parallel. The entire building is divided into construction sections covering different floors.

QUALITY MANAGEMENT

Quality

In building projects, quality refers to the contractually agreed condition of a building element after completion or installation. Along with schedule and implementation planning and monitoring costs, quality management is one of the three central tasks of site management. There are regularly disputes over whether building work is of the agreed quality and can thus be defined as free of defects. A fundamental cause of such disagreements has to do with the different ways in which the quality that has been agreed on is understood.

> ℘

DEFINING QUALITY

The quality required of a building and thus the required standard of work can be defined by the descriptions in tender specifications and plans or, once contracts have been signed, with reference to samples. In this context, it is important that descriptions are unambiguous and are understood in the same way by both the client and the contractor. The following points should be considered:

General descriptions

General descriptions such as "sound implementation," "correct work," and "top quality" cannot constitute the basis for an agreement because terms like "sound," "correct" and "top" are not clearly defined.

Special descriptions

Special descriptions such as those used in prospectuses or advertising can be defined as an agreed quality in so far as they offer unambiguous statements, e.g. fuel oil use 3 l/m^2 per year.

Hybrid descriptions

Hybrid descriptions require a concretization. For example, the term "durable covering" needs to be explained in terms of how long the surface can be expected to remain free of marks from wear.

Individual agreements

Individual agreements based on concretely defined aspects of the required results are always preferable to general descriptions.

℘

\\ Example:
If a client, an architect and a contractor are all asked what constitutes an acceptable "exposed concrete surface," they will give quite different answers. The client and the architect will expect a perfectly even surface free of color deviations and pores. The contractor, on the other hand, will insist that experience has shown that color deviations, pores, formwork joints, etc. cannot be avoided in even the most careful work and will therefore always be visible.

Sample

A sample presents an agreed level of quality and can be used as a guide in the implementation process.

The definition of the desired quality of a building element can take different forms. As already mentioned, descriptions of quality can be found, for example, in tender specifications, plans, sample reports, or photos. Table 6 shows how, for what purpose and with whom quality can be defined.

Tab.6:
Selected tools for reaching agreement on quality

Description of quality through:	Examples	Area of application, details of use	Problems and open questions
Production of samples	Textured plaster Facade coatings	Suitable wherever optical quality relies on craft skill.	Samples are often "too well" made and the same quality is not achieved on the actual surface.
	Hand-worked wooden surfaces Color transitions in natural stone floors and facades	Produce under building site conditions Carry out and document sampling Safeguard samples until final inspection of entire project.	Possible later deviations are often only vaguely described and cover a wide range
"Industrial samples" and their precise names	Paints e.g. RAL colors Sample stones Parquet blocks	Use among specialists possible. Very efficient in this context. Samples must correspond to the subsequent in situ use.	Small samples do not replicate the effect created in the finished space, which is difficult for laypersons to imagine.
Prospectus information and manufacturer supply catalogs	Switches and power sockets Heaters Toilet fixtures		

Description of quality through:	Examples	Area of application, details of use	Problems and open questions
Texts of functinal tender specifications	All construction work	Use among planners and implementing and planning contractors. Only partially comprehensible for client.	Specifications are described such that required functions are fulfilled. Implementation qualities are largely left to the contractor.
Texts of detailed tender specifications	All construction work	Use among planners and implementing contractors. Only partially comprehensible for the client.	Specifications must be described in detail since the description is also the basis for the contractor's cost calculations.
Comparable projects	e.g. as illustration of quality of exposed concrete	Very suitable when easily accessible. Shows already achieved quality	Accessibility and time needed for inspection
Sample spaces		Well suited to enabling laypersons to envisage elements in their spatial context.	Quality of sample spaces is usually "too good." Producing a sample space may be very costly.

Everyone on the building site is responsible for pointing out when a requested specification is objectively impossible.

Tenders/service specifications

All the qualities or characteristics desired by the client should be described in the service specifications is such a way that contractors are made clearly aware of the work they have to perform. Here, a distinction is made between detailed service specifications, which contain precise descriptions of the services required, and functional tenders, which contain descriptions of necessary functions or required features. The description of qualities and required services in service specifications includes:

_ Building specifications with general information on the building project

_ Contractual conditions

_ Planning documents (ground plans, sections, views)

_ Textual description of services with quantity information

_ Details of reference projects, samples and/or implementation examples

This information should be checked for completeness and validity by the site manager before work begins. In order to clarify the desired quality, the tasks described in the service specifications should be discussed with contractors before work commences in order to ensure that they have understood all requirements and are able to fulfill them.

Sampling inspection

In a sampling inspection the client is shown examples of building elements or implementation quality. Precise agreement on the quality of individual pieces of work is necessary above all in the case of visible surfaces and building elements. The surfaces and elements are subject to highly subjective assessment. The distinction between good and bad quality is dependent on and influenced by ideas, wishes and the observer's own craft experience and tastes.

Effects of the sampling inspection on costs and schedule

If a particular quality is specified or changed after a contract has been awarded, price changes will usually be made. Potential changes in cost and possible effects on the progress of building (different delivery times for alternatives) should be identified by the time of the sampling inspection so that these factors can be taken into consideration when making decisions.

Inspection list

It is easy to lose track of the agreements that are made, particularly in the case of large-scale inspections. For this reason, the results must be recorded in a report. It is advisable to draw up an inspection list of all

\\ Example:
An objective impossibility would be the construction of a 10 m long external plaster wall with a tolerance of 0 mm. Objective impossibility is understood as indicating that no one is able to build better.

\\ Tip:
If samples are produced, this should be done at the same pace and in the same way as on the building site. It is absolutely essential that the sample closely resemble what will later be featured on the building. If the finished work does not correspond to the sample (the latter is better) the client can demand implementation in accordance with the sample.

Administrative building for Müller AG		Sampling inspection result										XY architects
Item	Work section	Kamp-Lintfort	Herne	Dortmund	Haus Witten	Operational samples	Photos	Drawing	Status	Further sampling inspections	Cost increases/reductions	Notes
1	Facade											
1.1	Metal facade – aluminum	x							X			like KL
1.1.1	Lintel /window sill								X			RAL 7016
1.1.2	Panels – ceiling connector							x	X			as per agreement 12.03.03
1.2	Metal facade – steel			x	x			x	X			Sample 9006/9007 – 7016
1.2.1	Facade – canteen							x	X			as per agreement 12.03.03
1.3	Window system – office	x							X			like KL
1.4	Window system – foyer	x							X			like KL
1.5	Exterior sunshading – louver	x	x						X			like KL
1.6	Exterior sunshading – screen			x					-			No
1.7	Cylinder doors								-			No
	Vestibule / entrance								o			Decision by CW 15
2	Interior works											
2.1	Doors	x										
2.1.1	Doors – office areas	x										
	Architraves	x							X			like KL
	Door leaves	x							X			Wooden door leaves
2.1.2	Doors – conference rooms / canteen	x	x									
	Architraves	x	x						X			Metal architrave plates as wall connection
	Door leaves	x	x						X			Wooden door leaves depending on fittings
2.1.3	Doors – lobby / entrance	x										
	Architraves	x	x						X			OK like doors stairwell-office KL
	Door leaves	x	x						X			Steel-glass doors
2.2	Fittings	x	x						X			like KL
2.3	Glass panes	x	x						X			like KL
3	Metalwork											
3.1	Metalwork – interior finishing											
3.1.1	Stairs – foyer/canteen		x		x				X			System as in Witten
3.1.2	Handrails – stairs/gallery	x	x		x				X			As in KL, horizontal rods
3.2	Metalwork – shell											
3.2.1	Formwork – canteen			x					X			RAL 9006
3.2.2	F30 coating				x				X			Application as in paint shop
3.2.3	Enclosure BS/ventilation grills	x							X			"Waste room" KL OK similar
4	Floor											
4.1	Double-floor system	x							X			like KL
4.2	Floor covering											
4.2.1	Floor tiles/washrooms	x	x						X			like KL
4.2.2	Building stone – foyer	x							-			not applicable
4.2.3	Natural stone – foyer		x						X			as per agreement 12.03.03
4.2.4	Building stone – stairs	x	x						-			not applicable
4.2.4.1	Natural stone – stairs								X			aas per agreement 12.03.03
4.2.5	Parquet – canteen		x		x				-			not applicable
4.2.6	Floor tiles – food service					x			X			Sample as per costing
4.2.7	Floor tiles – kitchen					x			X			after agreement with StAfA
4.2.8	Carpet tiles – offices/conference room	x							X			like sample room
4.2.9	Linoleum BS rooms	x							X			like KL

x Sample as per costing
+ Sample more expensive than in costing

Status: Completed X
To be done o
Not applicable -

objects to be inspected and the above-mentioned effects that may ensue from changes. > Fig. 24

Fundamental sampling inspections should be undertaken before the contracts are agreed. Sampling inspections that do not affect costs (e.g. colors selected from a fixed palette of standard colors) can also take place during construction. > Chapter Cost management

MONITORING AND SAFEGUARDING QUALITY

When monitoring the quality of the building work, the site manager must pay particular attention to the following points:

_ Type and method of construction (particularly in the case of "damage-prone" types of work
_ Geometric quality (maintenance of dimensions, angles and levelness)
_ Optical quality (color, surface, uniformity)
_ Functional quality (functional efficiency of built-in elements)
_ Compliance with plans
_ Compliance with public regulations (building approval, ordinances and laws)
_ Compliance with manufacturer guidelines and standards

The site manager is especially required to directly monitor particularly complicated or damage-prone aspects of construction. These are aspects that experience has shown to involve a high risk of defects or cost increases.

Examples include:

_ Production of job-mixed concrete and semi-finished concrete elements (including armoring)
_ Sealing and insulation work
_ Relocation of drainage
_ Installation of ground pipes (integrity check)
_ Installation of building elements relevant to fire protection.

Supervisory duties

The site manager is responsible for the overall coordination of the building site but is not obliged to be constantly present on the building site and to supervise all work in detail. This applies particularly to the more simple and common building tasks. Examples include: plastering, laying flagstones, dry-construction of walls and ceilings and normal painting work. However, if any of this work proves defective, the site manager must engage more intensively in fulfilling his or her supervisory duties. A site manager must ascertain precisely whether the tradespeople on site have the skills to carry out the commissioned work and meet the agreed standards.

Technical specialists/ specialist engineers

Work on the building site should be supervised in a way that ensures that implementation corresponds to requirements. If the demands of this supervision exceed the expertise of the site manager, he or she must encourage the client to appoint technical specialists and specialist engineers. For some aspects of construction, the use of such expertise may even be prescribed:

_ Scaffolding
_ Building elements relevant to fire protection
_ Smoke and heat venting systems
_ Fire and smoke alarm systems
_ Building elements relevant to structural integrity
_ Elevator systems and escalators

The construction and installation of building services are usually supervised by a specialist site manager appointed by the firm responsible for the project's building services planning. This specialist is responsible for supervising the work of the firms commissioned with carrying out all building services work and ensuring this work meets the required standards. In the case of structural engineering elements, it is important that the responsible structural safety engineer is kept well informed about the progress of work so that he or she can monitor and document relevant stages of the work. When this work has been completed he or she must certify that it has been carried out according to regulations. These technical specialists must also be involved in the final acceptance and approval of these construction aspects. › Chapter Final inspection and acceptance

Dimensions and tolerances

The checking of geometric quality particularly concerns the dimensions of the ground plan and the heights as well as angles and evenness of building elements. If there are no specific agreements in the contract, established standards are taken as a guideline for implementation. Examples of permissible dimension deviations in the ground plan and ceiling heights are shown in Table 7. These examples refer to the German DIN Standard 18202 for tolerances in buildings.

The aim of establishing dimensional accuracy is to facilitate the functional assembly of elements of the shell and interior works without the need for adjustment and refinishing, despite the fact that inaccuracies are unavoidable in the production and fitting processes. It is important that the different work sections are relatively easy to integrate with one another. When limit values are exceeded, the work that follows has to be supplemented with measures to offset these mistakes.

Examples of permissible dimensional deviations in the ground plan and ceiling
heights in the building (based on DIN 18 202)

Dimension to be checked	Admissible tolerances (mm) for a nominal size of ...		
	up to 3 m	3 m to 6 m	6 m to 15 m
Lengths and widths in the ground plan	+ 12	16	20
Height between floors	16	16	20
Clear dimensions in the ground plan	16	20	24
Clear dimensions in the elevation	20	20	30
Openings (reveals without surface finishing)	12	16	–

LAWS/REGULATIONS/STANDARDS

There is a large body of laws and regulations governing the implementation and characteristics of building projects. Standards are established as a means of standardizing applications, characteristics and procedures and are formulated and published by organizations for standardization. In addition, professional associations and manufacturers provide instructions and guidelines for the use and handling of building products.

Recognized codes of practice

In the present context, recognized codes of practice are to be understood as rules applying to the construction of buildings and building elements. These rules are regarded both by scholars and practitioners as correct and have proved their worth over time.

Complying with the recognized codes of practice is assumed to be self-evident and not to require separate agreement in the contract. Building firms are responsible for keeping themselves informed of the currently recognized codes of practice. If these rules are not complied with then a defect is the result. › Chapter Quality management, Defects and defect correction A contractor can exclude liability for non-compliance if he or she agrees with the client not to comply with these rules and is properly informed about the possible consequences.

State of the art

State of the art refers to a higher stage of technological development than the recognized codes of practice but a stage that has not yet become established in practice in the longer term. Since particular value is placed on durability in the building field, only compliance with the recognized codes of practice is assumed in the construction field.

State of scientific and technical knowledge

The state of scientific knowledge represents the current state of research. This means that in the practical sphere there is very little or no experience of products and implementation forms based on the state of scientific knowledge. Applications of such knowledge in actual building practices are rare. An overview of these terms is given in Figure 25.

Standards

The roles of standards are manifold. They include acting as measures for rationalization, understanding, serviceability, quality assurance, compatibility, convertibility, health, safety, and environmental protection. Standards belong to the general technical specifications with which construction work has to comply. It should be noted that standards can become obsolete and may no longer necessarily accord with recognized codes of practice. For this reason recognized codes of practice take precedence over standards.

Guidelines/information/instructions

Apart from the technical principles already discussed that govern the way in which construction work is carried out, there are a range of guidelines and information that need to be taken into account when building:

_ Guidelines drawn up by professional associations
_ Manufacturers' instructions
_ Handling information
_ Mounting/installation instructions
_ Directions for use

Guidelines

In formal terms, a guideline is a prescription that is binding but not in a legal sense. Guidelines are issued by organizations such as trade associations (painters, roofers, wreckers, etc.) They are formulated on the basis of the relevant recognized codes of practice, standards, and practical experience. The respective guidelines are usually taken into account in agreements on how construction work is to be carried out.

Terms	Features			
	Scientific knowledge/ confirmation	Practical experience at hand	Generally known in professional circles	Established in practice
Recognized codes of practice	yes	yes	yes	yes
State of the art	yes	partly/ limited	partly	no
State of scientific and technical knowledge	yes	no	no	no

Fig.25:
Terminological structure of development levels of products and processes (based on Rybicki)

Handling in-
formation and
installation
instructions

Manufacturer's instructions, handling information, installation instructions and directions for use apply to individual building products and building elements and provide precise information, for example, on storage, use or installation. Information is also usually supplied regarding what other products can be used with the product in question. Site managers should inform themselves about the products used on their building sites to be able to check that their use is correct and free of defects.

\\Note:
Instructions are attached to many building products such as paints and glues, stipulating the minimum and maximum temperatures at which these products should be used. If they are used outside this temperature range, their effectiveness and durability is reduced.
Not all paints and glues can be used on all surfaces. Disregarding instructions in this respect can result in material failing to bond or one material damaging the other.

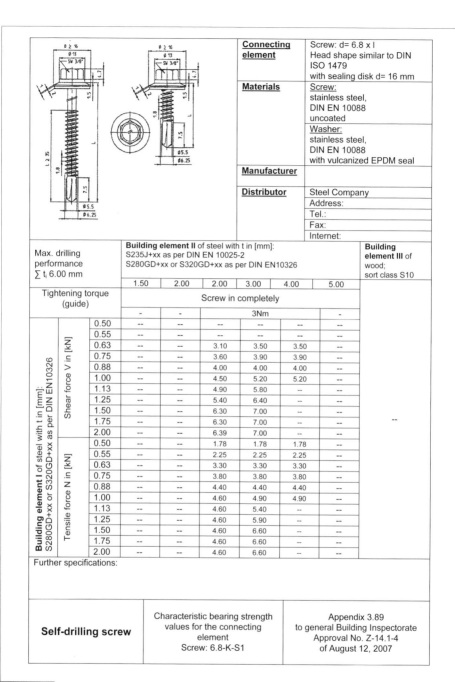

Connecting element	Screw: d= 6.8 x l Head shape similar to DIN ISO 1479 with sealing disk d= 16 mm
Materials	Screw: stainless steel, DIN EN 10088 uncoated
	Washer: stainless steel, DIN EN 10088 with vulcanized EPDM seal
Manufacturer	
Distributor	Steel Company
	Address:
	Tel.:
	Fax:
	Internet:

Max. drilling performance ∑ tᵢ 6.00 mm	Building element II of steel with t in [mm]: S235J+xx as per DIN EN 10025-2 S280GD+xx or S320GD+xx as per DIN EN10326					Building element III of wood; sort class S10
	1.50	2.00	2.00	3.00	4.00	5.00
Tightening torque (guide)	Screw in completely					
	-	-	3Nm			-

Building element I of steel with t in [mm]: S280GD+xx or S320GD+xx as per DIN EN10326

Shear force V in [kN]

	1.50	2.00	2.00	3.00	4.00	5.00
0.50	--	--	--	--	--	--
0.55	--	--	--	--	--	--
0.63	--	--	3.10	3.50	3.50	--
0.75	--	--	3.60	3.90	3.90	--
0.88	--	--	4.00	4.00	4.00	--
1.00	--	--	4.50	5.20	5.20	--
1.13	--	--	4.90	5.80	--	--
1.25	--	--	5.40	6.40	--	--
1.50	--	--	6.30	7.00	--	--
1.75	--	--	6.30	7.00	--	--
2.00	--	--	6.39	7.00	--	--

Tensile force N in [kN]

	1.50	2.00	2.00	3.00	4.00	5.00
0.50	--	--	1.78	1.78	1.78	--
0.55	--	--	2.25	2.25	2.25	--
0.63	--	--	3.30	3.30	3.30	--
0.75	--	--	3.80	3.80	3.80	--
0.88	--	--	4.40	4.40	4.40	--
1.00	--	--	4.60	4.90	4.90	--
1.13	--	--	4.60	5.40	--	--
1.25	--	--	4.60	5.90	--	--
1.50	--	--	4.60	6.60	--	--
1.75	--	--	4.60	6.60	--	--
2.00	--	--	4.60	6.60	--	--

Further specifications:

Self-drilling screw	Characteristic bearing strength values for the connecting element Screw: 6.8-K-S1	Appendix 3.89 to general Building Inspectorate Approval No. Z-14.1-4 of August 12, 2007

Fig.26:
Product data sheet for screws including technical details

Fig.27:
Label on glazing with technical
information and quality information

Delivery notes/labels/certification/data sheets

In order to find out whether the materials being used on the construction site meet the necessary requirements, site managers need to check delivered materials. The easiest way of doing this is to compare delivery notes and labels with the information in the building contract. The glazing material label shown in Figure 27 includes all required information:

_ Manufacturer
_ Firm/purchaser
_ Project
_ Glazing type and pane composition
_ Pane size
_ Quality certification

Site managers should collect all labels of important building materials and include them in the project documentation. If no precise specifications are available for material such as glazing, the required quality, or the quality deemed necessary by the recognized codes of practice, can be identified from quality certification or comparable information. It is also possible to request product information from the supplier. > Fig. 26 and Chapter Handover, Project documentation

DEFECTS AND DEFECT CORRECTION

Reworking, repairs, additional cleaning, and defect correction cost a lot of time and money and should be avoided where possible. Experience shows that the processes of identifying and documenting defects and monitoring their correction amount to approx. 10–15% of the site manager's work.

Defects

Defective work refers to work that does not meet set requirements or that deviates from the defined quality. Defects are divided into two categories:

Optical defects:

_ Dirt/stains
_ Minor damage
_ Color deviations
_ Unevenness
_ Minor cracking
_ ...

and constructional defects:

_ Cracking
_ Mechanical damage
_ Malfunctions
_ Spalling
_ ...

When assessing optical defects, the function and significance of surfaces must always be taken into account. The assessment must take place under conditions of normal use. This means, for example, that optical defects should be assessed from the same distance and under the same lighting as would apply when the object concerned was under normal use.

Defects are also distinguished in terms of the following categories:

An apparent defect is already present and discernable during construction or at the final inspection.

\\ Example:
_ Irregularities in the external appearance of a house (plaster, cladding) should be assessed from the street rather than from the scaffolding or lift trucks.
_ Irregularities on a front door should be assessed at the distance from which the door is normally seen.
_ Irregularities in the surfaces of a basement garage should be assessed under lighting conditions that will apply when the area is in normal use.
_ Focused light should be used for assessment only if such light is used regularly under normal conditions of use.

A hidden defect is present but not discernable at the final inspection.

Intentionally concealed defects are hidden defects that the contractor is aware of but deliberately does not mention at the final inspection in order to gain advantage.

To assess whether a defect is present, the following questions should be asked when assessing the work concerned:

_ Does the work exhibit the agreed quality?
_ Is the work adequate to the contractually assumed use of the product?
_ Is the work adequate to the normal use of the product?
_ Does the work comply with the recognized codes of practice?

In addition, the concept of a defect can also be applied to situations where

_ Fitting/installation has been incorrectly carried out
_ A product or delivery item is different to that which was agreed upon
_ Too little material has been delivered

Once defects have been identified, their significance needs to be assessed and a decision must be made as to what measures are appropriate.

Correction of a defect is required when the work in question does not comply with the recognized codes of practice, it is clear that further damage will result from the defect, or the required function is only partially fulfilled or not at all.

The distinctions drawn here make clear that not every defect must necessarily be corrected, since in some circumstances the effort and expense involved are not justified. In this case the defective work is "penalized" with a reduction in remuneration, i.e. a lower payment.

If the defect is within the range of agreed deviations, is located in peripheral spaces or is not visually significant, it is described as minor and

\\ Example:
Cladding in a basement or in a prestigious
entrance area, color deviations in the
flooring of a storage facility or in a
reception area, and unevenness in the interior
plastering of a stable or a living room have
to be assessed in different ways.

		Significance for functional reliability of building			
		Very important	Important	In-significant	Unimportant
Level of functional impairment	Very pronounced	Correction			
	Significant				
	Moderate			Mitigation	
	Marginal				Minor defects

Fig.28:
Possible consequences of functional defects

		Importance of appearance			
		Very important	Important	In-significant	Unimportant
Level of impairment to appearance	Conspicuous	Correction			
	Clearly visible				
	Visible			Mitigation	
	Barely visible				Minor defects

Fig.29:
Possible consequences of optical defects

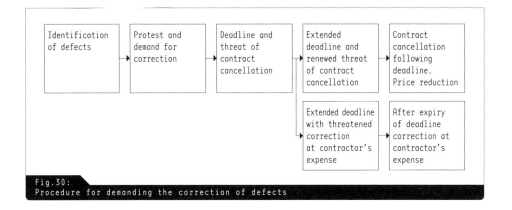

Identification of defects	Protest and demand for correction	Deadline and threat of contract cancellation	Extended deadline and renewed threat of contract cancellation	Contract cancellation following deadline. Price reduction
			Extended deadline with threatened correction at contractor's expense	After expiry of deadline correction at contractor's expense

Fig.30:
Procedure for demanding the correction of defects

does not have to be corrected. Figures 28 and 29 provide an overview of different consequences of defects. The point of departure is the degree to which the defect adversely affects the object or function concerned.

Work that is already recognized to be defective or contrary to contract during construction must be corrected by the contractor. Since the work involved in correcting defects is not paid for by the client, it can often produce considerable additional costs for the building firm. Defects must be corrected within an appropriate time period, which is defined by the client. The appropriateness of the time allowed is measured in relation to concrete conditions on the building site.

The contractor must be asked in writing to correct the defect. This is particularly important when only a limited amount of time is available for the correction (the project is nearing completion). Figure 30 shows a suitable procedure for demanding correction of defects.

\\ Example:
If the firm that has carried out defective work is still on the building site, the client can demand that the defect be corrected within a few days. If staff must be called back to the site, more time should be allowed. If subsequent work is directly dependent on the correction of the defective work, then speedy attention to the problem is expected on principle. If the contractor delays in correcting the defect, he or she can be made liable for additional costs relating to building delays.

67

COST MANAGEMENT

At the beginning of a building project, the client specifies the budget available. This budget forms the foundation of the planning phases and must be adhered to by the site manager during the building phase.

However, experience shows that building projects are very seldom completed for the price envisaged in the planning phase. Requested changes during the building phase, imprecisely calculated quantities and building elements that were overlooked during tendering can all lead to cost increases. The overview in the first chapter of cost developments during construction indicates which costs the site manager must maintain a focus on and, if necessary, manage. › Fig. 31

BUDGET

Planning includes determining the budgets that are to be allocated to the different service packages. Tenders are then called for and bids are compared with one another and with the budget. This initial tender vetting is important for the client since it shows whether the assumptions made during the planning phase actually correspond with the actual prices.

Tender vetting   Since tender vetting does not actually fall within the site manager's remit, it is only briefly discussed here. Tender vetting entails checking all bids for completeness and correctness and comparing them with one another. A range of computer programs designed for this purpose are available, although these comparisons can also be made using simple spreadsheets.

Once tenders have been vetted, public clients must award the contract to the lowest bidder. Private clients, on the other hand, are entitled to choose which bid they will accept.

At this point within the course of the project it is possible to influence costs. If the tendered sum exceeds or is below the estimated budget,

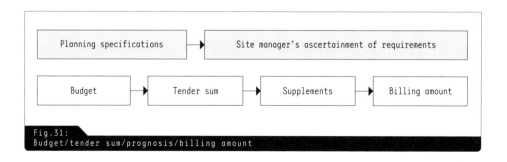

Fig. 31:
Budget/tender sum/prognosis/billing amount

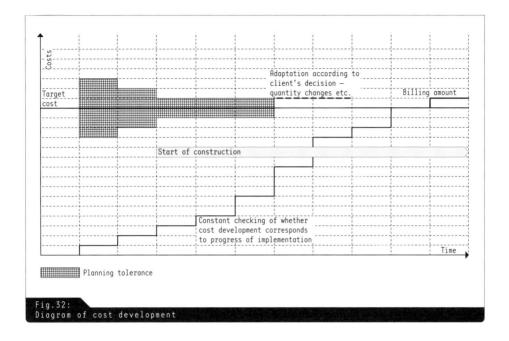

Fig.32:
Diagram of cost development

Legend within figure:
Costs
Target cost
Adaptation according to client's decision – quantity changes etc.
Billing amount
Start of construction
Constant checking of whether cost development corresponds to progress of implementation
Time
▦ Planning tolerance

then alternatives that have been put up for tender, i.e. simpler or higher quality variants, can be commissioned. › Fig. 32

TENDER SUM/CONTRACT SUM

Once a contract has been awarded to a building firm, the tender sum is fixed. Since private clients are free to negotiate bids with building firms, the contract sum is in some cases lower than the sum that was tendered and vetted. The negotiated reduction in such cases is referred to as an

Abatement

abatement. Usually it is agreed that the abatement will also apply to all subsequent contracts. Abatements for building contracts tend to range between 2% and 8%. In most countries, public clients are not permitted to negotiate bid prices.

PROGNOSIS, SUPPLEMENTS

Supplements

Supplements, i.e. bids for altered or additional work that exceeds the originally commissioned services, are submitted by the contractor. As a rule, supplements are formulated as bids on the basis of the agreed building contract. The additional work and related costs can be the result of:

_ Quantity variances
_ Changes to required services

_ Construction delays
_ Measures to speed up construction

In this context a distinction is made between:

_ Changes to building content (what is built differs from what was originally agreed)
_ Changes to building circumstances (the building complies with the original agreement but the construction circumstances change, e.g. the possibilities for access to the site are altered).

The effects of these changes can lead to an increase but also to a decrease in costs.

Supplement assessment

Before the services offered in the supplements are commissioned by the client, the site manager must assess whether the claims are justified. It must first be established whether the services offered as a supplement are not already included in the original building contract. If this is the case, the supplement will be rejected.

Original calculation

In addition, it is important to check whether the prices for the services being offered correspond to the price level of the building contract. To determine this, the site manager can compare and assess the prices on the basis of the contractor's original calculation. The original calculation shows the level of the original costing elements comprising the tender prices.

Supplements can be commissioned by the client alone. As already mentioned, the site manager is not permitted to make decisions for the client that may affect the client financially. For this reason, a supplement must be carefully examined and the client informed whether it is justified and whether the costs are appropriate.

Commissioning supplements

The examination and commissioning of a supplement should take place before the offered services are carried out. However, in practice it unfortunately often becomes clear only when construction is already underway that required services are not contained in the contract. At this point it is too late to wait for the supplement bid, the assessment and the client's approval in writing. However, in order to avoid interruptions to work, the client must be informed that additional costs are being incurred. Furthermore, the approximate costs should be submitted and discussed with the client. Given the client's approval, a preliminary commission can then be issued by way of a written report. In Figure 33 the relevant procedures are represented diagrammatically.

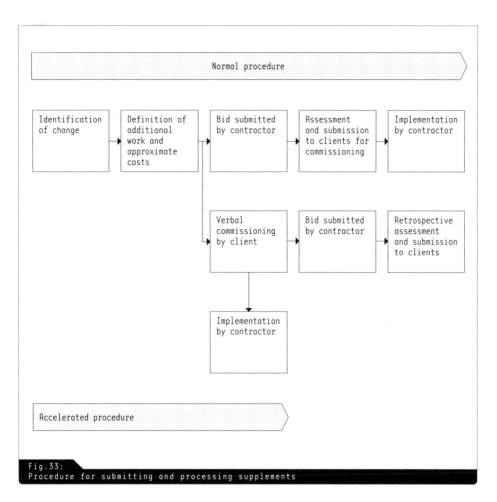

Fig.33:
Procedure for submitting and processing supplements

📎

\\ Note:

Although a site manager for the client only seldom handles the costing of contract works, he or she should be familiar with the structures involved.

The prices tendered by building firms usually comprise the following costing elements:

_ Costs for wages, building materials, tools and, if required, external services
- Costs incurred on the building site that are not included in the individual items of the tender
_ Costs for the contractor related to running and administering his or her firm
_ Costs for risks that are not precisely known but are shown by experience to be incurred due to construction delays, guarantees or unforeseen events.
_ The profit represents the estimate of the appropriate return on the capital invested by the contractor.

COST CONTROL

Cost control refers to the comparison of currently known costs with planned costs. At the time of construction, the site manager must compare the planned budget with the tender sums, including known supplements, and possible further costs (prognosis costs). If variances are noted, cost management measures must be taken. The first step in cost management in this context should be to look for potential savings in the affected work section in order to prevent other sections being affect. If possibilities for cost management here are insufficient, other budgets must be checked for means to cover the increased costs, or the client must increase the relevant budget.

COST MANAGEMENT

The further a project has progressed, the more difficult it is to exercise effective influence over costs. Even with careful planning and cost calculation, it can still be necessary to intervene in the development of costs. The site manager and the planner are then required to develop proposals for possible savings and calculate their feasibility and effects. As in schedule management, there are different possibilities here:

_ Changes in quality
_ Changes in quantities
_ Changes to the implementation schedule

In the case of all measures, it is important to consider that once a contract has been concluded the contractors may also be entitled to compensation for the services that have been dispensed with, since the calculation of tender prices is based on the quantities listed in the tender specifications. The savings that are actually made can only be identified in collaboration with the contractor.

Changes in quality
> 🛈

Changes in quality mean that the standards actually realized differ from those originally planned. This can mean that implementation is either of a lower or higher quality. Such changes are easiest to organize when the tender specifications already include alternative items.

However, it must always be kept in mind that the proposed changes can lead to additional costs in other areas.

Changes in quantities

Changes in quantities are often considered in association with changes in quality. Quantities can simply be reduced, or expensive variants can be limited to important areas and a simple standard applied to the rest.

Postponing work

There is also the possibility of postponing work, as long as the aims of the client permit this. This option is often used by private clients who are having single-family homes built. The attic or basement is fitted out or the garage is built several years after completion of the house.

The suggestions already made on how to manage schedule and implementation planning also apply to cost management. The desired effects on costs always exert effects on other aspects of the project. The site manager must always keep the following points in mind and provide adequate consultation for the client, who will often be unable to maintain the overview required to assess all effects.

_ What possible effects will changes have on schedules? Can the other materials be just as quickly delivered as the originally planned materials? Delaying completion can have a significant effect on costs.

_ Does the changed quality still meet the original requirements or does the more rapid deterioration of a cheap product mean that new costs will soon be generated?

_ What new costs are generated by later implementation?

_ What additional costs are generated by changing the existing building contract?

SETTLEMENT OF ACCOUNTS

The settlement of accounts for services performed, like the work itself, takes place in stages. Depending on the duration and scope of the work, settlement is made on the basis of an invoice, or made in stages over the period of work on the basis of part-payment invoices and the final account. Settlement of accounts for work thus usually takes place parallel to the progress of construction.

Invoices for construction services can only be submitted for work that has actually been carried out or for building material and elements that the contractor has demonstrably produced for the building site or already delivered but not yet installed.

In this case it is better to make an advance payment against a bank surety bond presented by the contractor.

>

\\ Note:
This procedure is common, for example, in
larger facade projects because the contractor
must purchase materials such as profiles,
glass, fittings and sealing material for the
manufacture of the facade elements and pay
suppliers. Otherwise the contractor would be
burdened with financing the period between
installation and final inspection.

Since the construction process generally lasts for a relatively long time, the contractor is entitled to demand payments on account, i.e. part payments, for services rendered on the building site.

Like the final account, each part-payment invoice must be verifiable. The invoice must therefore be accompanied by a list of the quantities relating to the services being invoiced, invoicing plans (listing what is to be invoiced) or a quantity survey.

Invoice verification entails establishing whether the invoiced work has actually been carried out and is largely defect-free. It must be carefully conducted because if the contractor becomes insolvent before the project is completed, the site manager will be liable to the client for possible overpayment for services rendered.

In order to determine the scope of services, a quantity survey is produced on the building site. This is particularly important for work that will later be concealed. This applies, for example, to sealing work that will later be concealed under flooring, demolition work, and repair work on walls that will be resurfaced later. Contractors have a particular interest in this work being surveyed since it may later be necessary to prove that the work has actually been carried out. › Final inspection Like invoices, quantity surveys must be clearly laid out and accord with the structure of the service specifications.

Accounting in this context refers to the form in which invoices are drawn up. The structure of the invoice should correspond to the structure of the service specifications. This makes it possible to maintain an overview of the costs of individual jobs and work sections in the course of cost control. If invoices are not structured in this way and are not clearly laid out, the site manager may reject them as being unverifiable.

Cumulative accounting has proved advantageous in the building industry. In a cumulative invoice, all services are invoiced that have been carried out up until the point of invoice submission. Services that have already been paid for are deducted.

Submission of these invoices must also include the relevant quantity survey sheets and invoicing plans. This type of accounting provides the site manager with an immediate overview of the work that has been done, the inclusion of quantity surveys means that a laborious examination of the overall quantity survey is not required when the final account is submitted. › Fig. 34

The final account includes all work carried out and includes agreed and commissioned supplements and quantity changes. Like part-payment invoices, the final account must be clearly laid out and easy to examine. The final account must be accompanied by the final quantity survey. This quantity survey is in principle based on the planning documents that also provide the foundation for the service specifications. In some cases a separate quantity survey on the building site can be required for altered services or services to which planning documents do not refer.

Site managers have a particular time frame for assessing invoices. In Germany this time frame is regulated by the terms of German construction contract procedures (VOB/B). These stipulate that final accounts must be paid within two months of submission. This only applies, of course, if the account is correct and verifiable. If this is not the case, the contractor must be informed within the two-month period. The same conditions apply to payments on account but the deadline is only 18 working days.

ρ
\\Example:
In the third part-payment invoice, the contractor includes all services rendered up until this point (including services from the first two invoices, which have already been paid) and refers them to the relevant items in the service directory. Any agreed abatement and a security deposit are deducted from the calculated amount. Payments relating to the first two part-payment invoices are also then deducted and the unpaid sum is calculated.

Invoice verification
(Cumulative accounting)

3. Müller AG ref.

Client:	**Vermögensanlagen West AG**	Building element:		
Building project:	**Demolition work**			
Job no.:	**450072820**	Project no.:	**D-06-0996**	Cost center: **Meier**
Title:		No.:		Contractor: **Müller AG**
Date of receipt:	**29.5.2007**	Date of invoice:	**24.5.2007**	Invoice no.: **VF-07-0252**

Verifiable? [X] Yes [ ] No   Reason:

[ ] Verifiable from date/reason:

		Not including VAT €	VAT 19% €	Incl. VAT €
1. Unverified amount		150'000.00		
2. Amount verified prior to deducting abatements		150'000.00		
3. Abatements	3.00 % (-)	4'500.00		
4. Value of work		145'500.00		
5. Security deposit	5% x 10% (-)	14'550.00		
6. Amount		130'950.00		
7. Value of prior payment(s)	(-)	90'000.00		
8. Amount		40'950.00		
9. Deductions (Charges as per appendix)	(-)			
10. Amount (value of payment)		40'950.00		
11. Discount	0.00 % (-)	0.00		
12. Amount due		**40'950.00**	7'780.50	**48'730.50**

Notes:

The invoiced sum corresponds to work performed.

Content   checked:

Calculation   checked:

Approved for payment:

Fig.34:
Sample form for a cumulative invoice assessment

FINAL INSPECTION AND ACCEPTANCE

ACCEPTANCE OF CONSTRUCTION WORK / TRANSFER OF RISK

The final inspection and acceptance of construction work or a building is carried out by the client and his or her representatives, i.e. the architect or site manager and the contractor. Final inspection can only take place once all work has been completely finished, with the exception of a few insignificant details. Final inspection can only be refused if particularly serious defects are evident that restrict the usability of the building or building element.

By undertaking a final inspection, the client formally recognizes that contracted work has been completed. In most countries inspection and acceptance are legally regulated. Contractors can demand inspection and acceptance of their work when it has been substantially completed. Final inspection involves checking that the services rendered correspond to contractual agreements. If the client confirms this to the contractor, the contract is regarded as fulfilled. If at this time works are known to be incomplete or defective and the client does not register any protest, the client has no subsequent claim to the correction of the defect or completion of work free of charge.

Every contractor is obligated to safeguard completed work up until final inspection and acceptance. If works are damaged prior to inspection, the party causing the damage is responsible for repairing it. If the responsible party cannot be identified, the contractor must repair the damage at his or her own cost.

\\ Tip:
If the site manager realizes that certain work has not been correctly carried out, he or she must inform the relevant contractors immediately and not wait until a partial or final inspection is being carried out. If the responsible parties are not informed immediately, potential damage caused by defective work may increase in the interim. Allowing a wall to be built while knowing that it is in the wrong position or that other work must first be completed ultimately only wastes time and money and causes stress. Having to demolish work that has just been completed has a very negative effect on worker motivation.

Depending on the type of building element, protection must be provided against, in particular:

_ Frost, rain and sun
_ Dirt
_ Premature or improper use
_ Mechanical damage
_ Theft

Hidden defects Intentionally concealed or hidden defects must be corrected by the contractor. Up until final inspection and acceptance, the contractor is responsible for protecting his or her work from damage, repairing any damage that does occur and submitting work according to contract.

Partial acceptance/final acceptance A distinction is made between partial acceptance and final acceptance. As pointed out in the discussion of part-payment invoicing and quantity surveys, partial acceptance can be carried out for individual services.

Inspection report If a defect is identified during the final inspection, this must be recorded in writing in the inspection report. › Fig. 35 The type and location of the defect must be described precisely.

Where there are differences of opinion, the contractor's objections must also be recorded in the report. The question of who should correct the disputed defect and who should pay for the work must be decided at a later date.

The legal consequences of acceptance can be summarized as follows:

_ Prior to acceptance, the burden of proving that construction work has been completed according to contract lies with the contractor. Following acceptance the client must prove that the defect has been caused by the contractor in question.

\\Tip:
Defects identified during the final inspection should be described in a report and marked on the ground plan drawings so that the relevant locations can be easily found when work done to correct defects is being inspected. The report and ground plan drawings must be attached to the overall inspection report and submitted to all parties involved.

REPORT   – PARTIAL ACCEPTANCE   ☐
                  – FINAL ACCEPTANCE   ☐

Project   :
Client   :
Date   :
Work section   :
Scope of inspection   :
Contractor   :
Contractor's representative   :
Architect's representative   :
BS representative   :
Client's representative   :
Defects   :

Separate defect list included as appendix ☐ ___pages/no separate defect list included ☐
No (visual) inspection approval given for listed defects.

Contractor will correct the defects in accordance with the contract _____ at the latest.

Inspection papers, instructions for service and maintenance, and documents prescribed by official regulations are

complete ☐/ are incomplete ☐/ are to be submitted subsequently ☐

The contractor will submit the missing documents by _____ at the latest.

Warranty period commences :

Warranty period concludes   :

Notes   :

Contractor objections   :

Signatures   :

_____   _____
Date/Contractor's representative   Date/Architect's representative

_____   _____
Date/BS representative   Date/Client's representative

The report consists of a total of ___ pages.

Fig.35:
Inspection report form

_ If defective work is accepted without protest, the client has no right to subsequent correction of the defect free of charge (except if the defect was hidden or deliberately concealed). Once work has been accepted, the warranty period begins.

_ The contractor can submit an invoice for the accepted work. Payment falls due.

Due to the significance of the acceptance process, the site manager must be well prepared for it. The following documents should be available at the time of inspection and acceptance:

_ Building contract with planning documents and service specifications
_ Reports of sampling inspections and other specifications
_ Lists or reports of defects noted at an earlier date and not yet corrected
_ Plans in which the identified defects can be recorded

WARRANTY

As already mentioned, acceptance also signifies the beginning of the warranty period, i.e. the period of time in which the contractor guarantees the contractually defined quality of the building element. Within this period, the contractor must correct, free of charge, defects for which he or she is responsible. This also applies to hidden and, in particular, deliberately concealed defects. Agreement on the duration of the warranty period can coincide with agreement of the building contract.

ACCEPTANCE BY REGULATORY AUTHORITIES

In addition to inspection and acceptance of construction works by the client, these works are also subject to an acceptance inspection by the relevant regulatory authorities. This inspection involves checking whether construction complies with legal and technical requirements and thus corresponds to the approved plans.

Building shell acceptance

Regulatory authorities must be informed when the building shell has been completed. As a rule, a building shell acceptance inspection is then conducted, during which structural integrity is checked as well as relevant sound and heating insulation and fire prevention aspects.

Final acceptance

Final acceptance takes place following completion of all work required for the construction of the building. The authorities must be informed of completion in writing. All documentation listed in the building permit as required for the acceptance inspection must be provided. This includes:

- Certification regarding heating and chimney systems
- Certification of fire prevention measures
- Certification that construction has been carried out by a specialist contractor

During the final acceptance inspection, the entire building is usually viewed and spot checks are made to ensure requirements have been met. Planning changes that have been made during the construction phase are checked by the regulatory authority and approved if they meet the required standards. Changes that do not meet these standards must be brought into line with the requirements stipulated by the building permit. Once the final acceptance procedure has been completed, the building is approved for use.

HANDOVER

HANDOVER TO THE CLIENT

The scope of the handover to the client depends on the size and complexity of the completed building. During the handover the client and parties who will later have responsibility for the building (building superintendent, facility manager) are instructed on the use of technical facilities and given the project documentation. › Chapter Handover, Project documentation

The structure of the handover procedure should be divided into subject areas that reflect the division of work sections during construction. This facilitates proper instruction of the relevant parties. These areas can be defined as follows:

_ Building in general
_ Constructional fixtures and fittings such as doors, dividing walls and built-in furniture
_ Furniture and specific building equipment
_ Facades and facade engineering
_ Fire prevention features
_ Building services in general

Or, if necessary, divided into building services work sections

_ Heating engineering
_ Ventilation engineering
_ Sanitary engineering
_ Electrical engineering
_ Media engineering
_ Computing
_ Communications engineering
_ Safety engineering

These instructions should be given by the site manager and the planners responsible for the individual sections. All project documentation must be submitted when the handover to the client takes place.

PROJECT DOCUMENTATION

It is important for the client that he or she receives all documentation relevant to the building in an orderly form. Experience shows that this is also in the interests of the site manager since otherwise the client must consult him or her on every question arising after occupation of the building. Structured building documentation should include the following documents:

- _ Index of all documents
- _ List of planners involved in the project and contact persons
- _ Contact persons for warranties
- _ Building permit with acceptance reports
- _ Building shell documentation and acceptance reports
- _ Interior finishing documentation including acceptance reports, log books, records of materials used, instructions for use, maintenance instructions, etc.
- _ Facade documentation including planning documents, log books, inspection papers, records of glazing, profile and other materials, sun-protection inspection documents, etc.
- _ Documents relating to building services works including planning documents, acceptance reports, technical descriptions, inspection papers, log books, etc.

Log books are provided by manufacturers for equipment and fittings that require regular inspections, e.g. elevators, automatic doors, automatic fire protection equipment, and air-conditioning and ventilation systems. The site manager should draw the client's particular attention to stipulations on the regularity of inspections. Failure to comply with such stipulations can result in a loss of claim to warranty and premature deterioration. The maintenance and servicing of large and complex buildings is a time-consuming and labor-intensive process, and today specialized facility management firms are commonly engaged to carry out this work.

APPENDIX

PICTURE CREDITS

Figures 14, 15 and 32:	after Ulrich Nagel
Figure 28 and 29:	Rainer Oswald
Table 3:	Bert Bielefeld
All other figures:	The author

THE AUTHOR

Lars-Phillip Rusch is a freelance architect and research associate with the Department of Construction Management at the Dortmund University of Applied Sciences.

The author would like to particularly thank Professor Ulrich Nagel for making available textual and pictorial material that contributed significantly to this book.

Series editor: Bert Bielefeld
Conception: Bert Bielefeld, Annette Gref
Layout and Cover design: Muriel Comby
Translation into English: Joe O'Donnell
English Copy editing: Monica Buckland

Library of Congress Control Number: 2007936131

Bibliographic information published by the German National Library
The German National Library lists this publication in the Deutsche Nationalbibliografie; detailed bibliographic data are available on the Internet at http://dnb.d-nb.de.

This book is also available in a German language edition (ISBN 978-3-7643-8085-4).

© 2008 Birkhäuser Verlag AG
Basel · Boston · Berlin
P.O. Box 133, CH-4010 Basel, Switzerland
Part of Springer Science+Business Media

Printed on acid-free paper produced from chlorine-free pulp. TCF ∞
Printed in Germany

ISBN 978-3-7643-8104-2
9 8 7 6 5 4 3 2 1   www.birkhauser.ch

Also available from Birkhäuser:

Design
Basics Design and Living
Jan Krebs
978-3-7643-7647-5

Basics Design Ideas
Bert Bielefeld, Sebastian El khouli
978-3-7643-8112-7

Basics Design Methods
Kari Jormakka
978-3-7643-8463-0

Basics Materials
M. Hegger, H. Drexler, M. Zeumer
978-3-7643-7685-7

Fundamentals of Presentation
Basics CAD
Jan Krebs
978-3-7643-8109-7

Basics Modelbuilding
Alexander Schilling
978-3-7643-7649-9

Basics Technical Drawing
Bert Bielefeld, Isabella Skiba
978-3-7643-7644-4

Construction
Basics Facade Apertures
Roland Krippner, Florian Musso
978-3-7643-8466-1

Basics Loadbearing Systems
Alfred Meistermann
978-3-7643-8107-3

Basics Masonry Construction
Nils Kummer
978-3-7643-7645-1

Basics Roof Construction
Tanja Brotrück
978-3-7643-7683-3

Basics Timber Construction
Ludwig Steiger
978-3-7643-8102-8

Professional Practice
Basics Project Planning
Hartmut Klein
978-3-7643-8469-2

Basics Tendering
Tim Brandt, Sebastian Th. Franssen
978-3-7643-8110-3

Urbanism
Basics Urban Building Blocks
Thorsten Bürklin, Michael Peterek
978-3-7643-8460-9